YESTERDAY'S BOYS

BOYS

A Memoir

John Echols

Jan-Carol
Publishing, Inc

"every story needs a book"

Yesterday's Boys
John Echols

Published January 2023
Heirloom Editions
Imprint of Jan-Carol Publishing, Inc.
All rights reserved
Book Design: Tara Sizemore

ISBN: 978-1-954978-73-7
Library of Congress Control Number: 2023930433

You may contact the publisher:
Jan-Carol Publishing, Inc.
PO Box 701
Johnson City, TN 37605
publisher@jancarolpublishing.com
www.jancarolpublishing.com

My grandmother, Rosa Ellen Trent,
without her this book would not be possible.

Author's Note

I grew up 16 miles back in the mountains from the town of Grundy, Virginia, in a small coal mining hollow called Patterson. This book is a true collection of things that happened in the 1950s and 1960s. Hopefully this book will shed some light on the good times and bad times, and preserve a small bit of history from that era for the younger generations.

To

Ires

one of my favorite ladies in

Key West today. Thank you

JE 6-5-23

Table of Contents

Rosa Ellen Stanely Trent
"Maw"
(May 22, 1897–January 1976)

Maw was my maternal grandmother. Without her presence in my life as I was growing up, I am uncertain of what my future would have been. Maw was dirt poor with no income when we came to live with her.

She had married Thomas Lennox Trent in July 1913. Ten children were born to this marriage. Two of the children died very early in their lives. She and my grandfather were raising the other eight children when my grandfather became ill in 1946 and died at the age of 52.

There were five of the eight children still living at home. There were no benefits of any kind at that time to help her with the remaining children. Of course, there was no insurance or anything else that could have assisted. She provided for the children till the time they left the home. In addition, we had all moved in with her. There was no income, and we never went to bed hungry.

The eight children were Cleo, Hattie Patricia ("Pat"), Ethel ("Ett"), Geneva ("Boots"), Cecil ("Dick"), Thomas Jr. ("Tom"), Donald ("Harry"), and Jacklyn ("Jackie").

All are now deceased. Jacklyn was the last to pass and died in January 2022.

Maw was the kindest person you could ever meet. She helped any person or any animal that needed assistance in any way. She always provided and never complained about her hard life. She was kind, compassionate, strong-willed, and a survivor.

Patterson, Virginia

This book was written to try and shed some light on the good times and bad times of growing up in the coal mining community of Patterson, Virginia in the 1950s and early '60s. Sometimes referred to as the "holler," Patterson is located 16 miles back in the mountains from the town of Grundy, which is the county seat of Buchanan County.

There wasn't any earth-shattering history made there, but it is our history—good or bad, we lived it. I am not ashamed of it; in fact, I am proud of it. Some of the names have been changed to protect the guilty, the innocent, and all in between, but mostly the guilty.

Most of the old people that lived in the holler have passed on. Many kids that I went to school with have also passed on. If it wasn't for many of them, this book could not have been written. Rest in peace.

These chapters try to capture some of the things that happened and stand out in my memory. This book is about 85% true and about 15% not quite so. After about 60 or 70 years, my memory is a little fuzzy around the edges—some things like who was there, how far it was, the price of a ticket, and some of the smaller details. Nothing major. If I live long enough to go back to my second childhood, I will correct all the mistakes in this book.

Patterson was a small coal mining community with about 50 houses. Most were owned by the Sycamore Coal Company. They also owned the coal mine, company store, and boarding house. Also, the coal company owned the only telephone within a 10-mile radius. All the company houses were painted yellow and green.

If you were in Grundy and wanted to go to Patterson, you would go east on Route 460 out of Grundy for about 10 miles. The road would fork at the Dismal Bridge. The right fork was 460 East toward Richlands, and the left fork was Route 638. Continue on Route 638 and go about 3 miles till the road forks again. Route 638 will continue toward Crystal Block and is the right fork. The left fork goes toward Patterson and is Route 641. Another mile or so, and a house appears on the side of the hill, then another and another. The blacktop road is on the left, the creek in the middle, and the N & W Railroad is on the right.

A little further up the road on the left is the company store. On the right across the creek and railroad is the tipple where coal was processed and put in railroad cars. Farther up the holler about a quarter of a mile is the boarding house. About a quarter of a mile more, and the blacktop stops. It is then a dirt road. The railroad ended where the blacktop also ended.

Continuing up the road are a few more houses scattered here and there. The farther you go, the road becomes narrower. It goes all the way to the head of the holler. Then, the road crosses over the top of the mountain and down the other side for about 2 miles and ends at the Slate Creek Post Office.

There isn't much level land in Patterson. The best way to describe it is, it is shaped like a V. There are steep mountains on both sides, and at the bottom of the V is the road, creek, and railroad, with houses stuck on the sides of the mountains. I hope you get a little bit of the picture of what the holler looked like.

Please keep in mind that this is being written by a hillbilly boy that flunked 10th grade English. A passing grade was 70 and I had a 69 average. The teacher wouldn't give me 1 point. It was a big deal to me at that time, but not so much now. Thank you anyway, Mrs. Bevins.

Life in Patterson was simple back then. Most everyone in the holler was poor. We just didn't know how poor. I think for the most part, everyone was happy, or maybe that's just because I was a kid at the time.

You could go off and leave your house or car unlocked for a week and no one would take anything. If someone had some bad luck or got in a tight spot and needed some money, then someone would come through and loan it to them. When payday came, they would always get their money back.

There wasn't any crime of any kind that I can remember. Patterson was a good place to grow up.

We were all proud to be American. We were all hillbillies, and we were proud of that. Many southern people didn't have many material things. But they had, and still have, a hell of a lot of pride.

This is how I got lucky enough to be raised in Patterson. My mother's name was Ethel, but my sister, Sue, and I always called her "Ett."

My father was an alcoholic 24/7. Any time he had money, he was drunk. Sometimes he would come home so drunk, he would attempt to sit down, miss the whole chair, and land in the floor.

Usually, when my parents would physically fight, it would be two licks. Daddy would hit Ett, and she would hit the floor. I remember one night, he hit Ett so hard she landed in a corner of the living room. It took her a long time to get up.

Occasionally, he would have the DTs (delirium tremens) very bad and was unable to do anything. He would put a towel around his neck, get one end of the towel in his left hand and the other end in his right hand with a cup of coffee in it. Then, he would pull the towel down with his left hand until the cup got to his mouth.

When he was financially broke, which was all the time, he would sell anything he got his hands on to get enough money to buy a fifth of Four Roses Bourbon. My mother had a Kodak camera, and it was the only thing she owned that had any monetary value. She kept it hidden. Daddy found the hiding place and took the camera to town and pawned it for enough money to buy a fifth. As soon as Ett found out about it, she borrowed enough money to get it out of hock and hid it again. Daddy never found the hiding place again. My sister still has the camera today.

Daddy worked at the Crowell Chevrolet Garage in Iaeger, West Virginia. It was owned by C. C. Francisco, and he was married to my dad's sister, Vinny, but everyone called her "Boo." They owned several dealerships in West Virginia. The dealerships were in Iaegar, War, Welch, Bradshaw, and one more, but I can't remember where.

That was probably the only way my dad could keep his job. I'll give him credit; he worked every day drunk or sober, and he was very good at what he did. He was a car body repairman. He worked in the basement in the body shop of the dealership in Iaegar.

All this drinking, fighting, no money to pay the bills, and trauma every-day took its toll on my mother. She had a nervous breakdown. Everything went to hell then. Nothing would be the same. Ett and Daddy got a divorce.

After the divorce, my mother, sister, and I bounced around from aunt to uncle to grandmaw. Sometimes, my sister was with one relative, and I was with another. We didn't know where we would be next week. When a family is separated by divorce, it is very hard on the kids. It leaves scars that last a lifetime. They aren't visible with the naked eye, but they are still there. After a couple of years of bouncing around, in and out of schools with no permanent home, we finally landed at my grandmaw's house.

The good Lord was smiling on us that day. Thank you, Lord! Everything was good after that. Grandmaw did not have any money, but we didn't need money —we needed a stable family life. I needed to know if I would be sleep-ing in the same bed next week as I was sleeping in tonight. This is how I came to be raised in Patterson.

Many kids do not know how blessed they are. Ett never really recovered. She was in and out of hospitals the rest of her life. My daddy's addiction put my mother in an early grave. She was 56 when she died. It affected my sister, Sue, much more than me, but it didn't do me any good either.

Four-Room School

Once we got settled down, we started school. The four-room school I attended was Patterson Elementary. All the students, grades 1-7, attended this school. First and second grades were in one of the four rooms. Third and fourth grades were in another one of the rooms. The next room housed the fifth and sixth grades. In the fourth room was the seventh grade. After the completion of the seventh grade, you caught a school bus to Grundy to complete your education.

The school was a long wooden building that had been painted white. There were huge windows, and each window had about 40 smaller panes in it. Four chimneys came out of the roof—one chimney for each room. No central air or heat existed. Each of the four rooms had their own Burnside wood/coal stove.

At the front of the school, there were two sets of steps, each leading to their own small porch. From the porch, you stepped inside a smaller room about 8' x 8'. Then, there was a door to the right and one to the left. If needed, the two center rooms opened to one large room. Each room had several blackboards. The school building had a tin roof. On each end of the school building about 100 feet away were the outhouses. There was one on each end of the building—one for the girls and another one for the boys.

Mr. Perkins was the school principal. Every morning he would step out on the porch and ring the bell to signify school was in session. He rang it again at 12:30 indicating lunch was over. One more time in the evening, and school was over. I don't remember him ever missing a day of school. We couldn't have been so lucky. I think he was from North Carolina.

Most every morning, around 10:00 a.m., he would go to the outhouse and stay for about 30 minutes, or however long it took to smoke two cigarettes. After he had his nicotine fix, he would come back to the building. On his way back, he passed by the windows to see if we were talking. When he entered the room, he would start screaming at us saying how stupid or how ignorant we were. He had two favorite things to say. One was, "You darn little hillbillies, I'll mop the floor with you!" The second rant was, "You darn little hillbillies, if you fell down, your head would sprout for onions!"

If he kept on ranting and raving at us, he would get worked up even more. We knew what was coming next. He would holler, "Line up!" Everyone would line up single file in front of his desk, and he would give us a whipping. After you got your dose of medicine, you went back to your seat and did not say a word. This happened regularly. I stood in that line many times.

One girl in our class was named Linda. She was very slender and wore thick glasses. She was a very nervous person. Mr. Perkins would holler at her every chance he got. He would stand beside her desk and go on and on until she was in tears. I really felt sorry for her. Thank the Lord she passed the seventh grade. The next year, she would go to Grundy.

Each room had a wood and coal stove in it. I think the name of the stove was Burnside. They got the name right. If you stood close to one side, you would burn up on that side and freeze on the other.

There was an annual contract to build fires in all four stoves each day in the winter. I think it paid $15.00 per month. I would have killed to get the contract. $15.00 was a great deal of money. But I never got it.

On each stove, there was a coffee can full of water to put moisture in the air. One morning before school started, one of us boys got a bright idea to pee in the coffee can. After an hour or so, when it got hot, it started to stink. It wasn't overwhelming, but it was definitely in the air.

The teacher's name was Mrs. Love. She started looking little by little. She looked in all four corners of the room and under everyone's desk. She thought someone had peed in their pants. She would go outside and leave the door open. She couldn't leave it open too long because it was cold outside. She went and got Mr. Perkins. He came down and looked here and there, but he couldn't find the problem either. Later in the day after it had all evaporated, the smell gradually disappeared.

If we had gotten caught, there would have been hell to pay. We didn't try that trick again. We got away with it once, and we didn't push our luck. Mr. Perkins' room did not need a coffee can. As much as he ranted and screamed, I am sure there was plenty of moisture in the air all the time.

We had one teacher. I think she taught the fifth and sixth grades. She always gave the kids a lot of homework. If you didn't have it finished and turned in the next morning, you got a minimum of 10 licks with her famous paddle.

The paddle was varnished and polished with a high gloss. There was white hospital tape on the handle so it didn't slip out of her hand.

When you got a paddling from her and she hit you with the first lick, you knew she meant serious business, and you were on the business end. After 10 or more licks, you knew you had a paddling. From there on, you put a little more effort into your homework.

My sister was a couple of years ahead of me in school. About two or three years ago, I asked her if she remembered the fifth-grade teacher and her paddle. She said she sure did; she got a paddling from her, and her butt was sore for a week.

Every one of us kids was afraid of her. Everyone in the fourth grade knew what was coming the next year. Have you ever heard the phrase, "Show me the love?" Well, she would show you what love was all about. Her name was Mrs. Love.

Growing up in the holler and going to that four-room school for seven years was bad enough, but some of us spent a year or two more there before we escaped.

I am surprised some of us did very well for ourselves.

It is a miracle we all didn't get jobs in Chinese laundries picking farts out of underwear.

The politicians started a hygiene campaign for the Appalachian school kids. I think it was all BS to help someone get elected. About two or three times a week, Mr. Perkins would pass out a questionnaire about your hygiene. The very first question was, "Did you take a shower this morning?" The only shower in the whole holler was at the miner's bath house. We were lucky to have hot water to wash our face. "Did you comb your hair this morning?" "Did you brush your teeth this morning?" One of the girls in class always read the question and answered it incorrectly. She always checked the "yes" box. But you could tell she hadn't brushed her teeth in a month.

Every day, my grandmaw made me take my toothbrush and a glass of water out in the yard, rain, shine, or freezing cold to brush my teeth. I still have good teeth today. Thank you, Maw.

Do you know how we know a hillbilly invented the toothbrush? If anyone else had invented it, it would be called a "teethbrush."

In school, I would always sit by the window, and from where I sat, I could see the railroad. Many, many days I would see the steam engines bring the empty coal cars up in the holler, drop them off, hook onto the loaded coal cars, and leave. It was nice to daydream for a few minutes and wave at the engineer. He would always wave back.

Concert & Cake Walk

The little four-room school in Patterson was always strapped for money. Mr. Perkins was always looking for ways to make a little extra cash. Therefore, Mr. Perkins would have two or three concerts every year with country music stars. Many stars were from the Grand Ole Opry. Everyone in the holler would get excited. We were going to get to see a Grand Ole Opry star in person and up close. The tickets were maybe 50 cents for the school kids and $1.50 for the adults or maybe a little more. That was a big deal for all of us. We got to see stars like Lester Flatt, Earl Scruggs, Bill Monroe, Ralph Stanley, Tom T. Hall, and a few more. If it had not have been for these concerts, we never would have gotten to see these people.

There weren't any TVs in the holler at that time, so everyone listened to them on the radio on the Grand Ole Opry, Saturday Night Jamboree, and Wayne Rainey and his harmonica. I don't think we ever got to see Minnie Pearl. We can't forget we were listening to WNRG in Grundy, Virginia. These concerts put a face to the music that we heard on the radio. I wish I had saved the advertisement posters that were on the telephone poles for miles around. Some of them had autographs. Hindsight is always better than foresight.

A couple of times a year, Mr. Perkins would have a box supper and a cake walk. These were also to raise money for the school. Any lady that wanted to participate would pack a lunch, put it in a box or bag, take it to the school and put it on the table with the rest of the boxes. The boxes were auctioned off to the highest bidder. The winner would get to eat it with the lady who packed it. Some of the bids on the boxes went rather high. On the same night, they would have a cakewalk. The ladies would make their favorite cake and bring it to the school. Some of these cakes looked really good.

The cake walk was a little different with a line drawn on the floor. Anyone who wanted to get in paid his money, which was about 50 cents. A single guy or girl and guy got in line and formed a big circle. The music started and everyone walked around in a big circle. When you got close to the line on the floor, you would hope the music would stop. The person playing the music was not supposed to look. The music would play for a while and then it would stop. Everyone would stop. Then, whoever was behind the line or the next one to step over the line was the winner. I always saved my money until the German Chocolate Cake was the prize. I paid my money and got in line. When the music stopped, I always walked away empty handed. No German Chocolate Cake for me. Usually, two or three people would cut the cake they won and share. I usually got a piece or two.

Halloween Party

One year, Mr. Perkins decided to have a Halloween Party at the school. He tried to generate a little money. The school room was decorated and there would be games to play, which cost about 10 or 15 cents.

There were food and drinks for sale. No alcohol was allowed. We decorated one room like a haunted house. It was dimly lit with candles, skeletons, and pumpkins here and there while spooky music played.

There was a path through the room once you paid for a ticket and started. There was no turning back. My job was to hide under a desk. I had a quart jar filled with ice water to get my hands cold. When the ladies and girls would slowly walk past, I would reach out and put my hands on their ankles. Every time I touched one, they would scream to the top of their lungs and do a dance trying to get away. After a while, I got brave, and when I grabbed their ankle, I would run my hand up their calf to about their knee. They always screamed and turned the two-step into the jitterbug. I was having a great time. I must have gotten carried away. After a while, Mr. Perkins came in and told me to only touch their ankle. It was good while it lasted. I think the ladies got a thrill out of it. I guess you could say they got a kick out of it.

One Halloween, some of the boys decided to pass out treats to the first and second grades at school. At that time, there was a laxative that looked like chiclets chewing gum. It was called "Feen-A-Mint." There was another one that looked like small squares of Hershey chocolate bars. I don't how much they passed out, but the next school day, there were only about four or five kids that showed up for school.

Schoolbooks

In the '50s, very seldom did any of the kids buy new schoolbooks. New books were very expensive. We always tried to take the cheapest route. At the end of the school year, you would sell your books and use that money to buy next year's books. If you were lucky, you would break even.

I always tried to buy my books from someone who underlined the important stuff. That kind of gave me a little help during the next school year. Lord knows I could have used some help, especially in English. I am sure you have noticed by now.

Things were extra bad one year; the mine was only working one or two days a week. Things got very tight. That year, I sold my books to one kid. His family, just like all the other families in the holler, had no money. They paid me with vegetables out of their garden.

All of us kids didn't realize how tough things were. Cash money was hard to find.

We all survived.

James and Joe

I had two friends—James and Joe. Their fathers worked at the Sycamore Coal mine in Patterson. They lived about a ¼ mile up the road from me. One day, I was walking up to their house. About halfway up, I heard a commotion coming from down the mountain.

James and Joe were gathering apples. They were about 200 feet from where I was standing. They couldn't see me, but I could see them.

Jake Smith had a small apple orchard. James and Joe were right in the middle of it. Jake must have been taking a nap or wasn't home because he didn't let anyone in the orchard.

I decided to throw a rock and try to scare them, but there was no way I could throw a rock that far. I looked around and found a piece of slate about the size of a fifty-cent piece. Slate is a byproduct of coal mining, usually gray, flat, smooth, and sometimes thin. The piece I found was ideal for sailing. I threw it as hard as I could. I played a lot of ball so I could throw pretty good. The rock went straight out, and it kept going and going. It started falling slowly, and it kept on going slow and falling. It went so far, I could not see it anymore. A few seconds later, I heard a bloodcurdling scream. I hit James in the head just above his ear. Am I in trouble now! I got down there in record time. When I first saw him, he had blood all over him. It scared the crap out of me. I thought he was going to bleed to death. After his mom got the bleeding to stop and cleaned it up, the cut didn't look too bad. I told him and his mom about a dozen times that I was sorry. I was sorry. I felt bad, but probably not as bad as James felt.

We were still friends after that and remained friends for years and years. I was sure glad I did not hit him in the eye.

A few weeks later, he got even with me plus interest—unintentionally, of course. During the summer, we all went barefoot. No one had money for summer shoes.

We were going to pitch some horseshoes. That was one of the games we played a lot. Once you had a set of shoes and two pegs, you were in business. From then on, it didn't cost anything. That was all we could afford.

We measured off 40 feet, drove the pegs in the ground, and let the games begin. Joe and I played against James and Tommie.

The game was going very good, Joe and I were winning by a mile. Then, it all went downhill quick. The next one James pitched hit the top of the peg and glanced off. The very next thing it hit was my big toe. About half of my big toenail disappeared in a heartbeat. If I would have been there by myself, I would have cried. But you can't cry in front of all your friends.

It hurt like hell, and it sure felt good when it quit hurting. My toe swelled up and looked awful. If I would've had a pair of summer shoes, I wouldn't have been able to wear them for a month. My toe healed up by the time school started, so everything was good. The next time I pitched horseshoes, I did not stand behind the peg.

There is one more little escapade with the brothers, and then we will move on. One day, James, Joe, and I each had a nickel. I can't recall how we each had a nickel a piece. We'd probably hoed someone's garden or cut some firewood. The main thing is we had a nickel each, and it was burning a hole in our pockets.

I wouldn't buy pop at the time because they raised the price from five cents to six cents. This was entirely too much money, so I swore I would never buy pop again. At that time, we all drank R.C. (Royal Crown Cola). It was the biggest bottle you could get for a nickel. This was my first encounter with inflation.

We decided to buy a poke of Beech Nut Chewing Tobacco. It was exactly 15 cents a poke.

We went down to Limbach's store, and James made the purchase. We were on our way now.

James was older and bigger than me, and Joe was younger and smaller than me. James told us to take what we wanted because he was going to take the rest. Determined to get my nickel's worth, I stuffed all I could in my jaw. Then, I stuffed a little more.

Joe stuffed all he could get in his jaw, and James took the rest. Everything was going well. I was chewing with the big boys now. Chew and spit, chew and spit. About an hour to an hour and a half later, I began to feel a little sick. Then, I began to feel real sick. I mean, SICK!

I think I turned green. On a sick scale of 1 to 10, I was a 12 and climbing. I threw up everything in my stomach. I think I threw up stuff that I hadn't eaten yet.

I threw up again and again. Then, the dry heaves started, over and over. I think I was sick for hours and hours. I don't remember how long I was sick, but the sick time was a lot longer than the chew time. I got a lot more than a nickel's worth for that nickel.

That was the first and last time I chewed tobacco. The smell of it to this day almost makes me sick. Looking back, that nickel was very well spent. It saved me a lot of money and my teeth.

Break-In

About 11 o'clock one night, all of us kids were sitting around the kitchen table "tee-heeing" and "ha-haing." Anything to keep us from going to bed. Some of us were having a hillbilly dessert—crumbled cornbread in a glass of sweet milk. When you eat this, you must be very careful or you will get choked easily.

My cousin, Betty, had just made herself a sandwich. The laughter and carrying on came to an abrupt halt. We heard someone on the back porch. Then, they walked across the porch, shook the doorknob, and walked back across the porch. No one should've been on our porch at 11 o'clock at night. This was the middle of the night for us.

Then, whoever it was came back across the porch and shook the door-knob again.

We were all scared to death. We all decided we better get Maw and tell her what was happening. She was dead asleep. She would go to bed about the same time the chickens go to bed—"real early." Three or four of us kids woke her up and proceeded to tell her someone is trying to break in. It took her a few minutes to get the picture. She had on her night gown and night cape. She got up, opened the nightstand drawer, and retrieved her trusty .38 Smith and Wesson revolver.

By now, she was a little nervous. She attempted to put one bullet in, and it fell out. Finally, she got six bullets in the revolver. The gun was ready now.

She went trapsing through the house holding the gun out in front of her, all of us kids following along behind. She went through the house a couple of times and concluded no one was in the house. After about an hour, Maw decided everyone was safe. So, she went back to bed. We all decided we would go to bed. We'd had enough excitement for one night. The next day, after a couple of hours discussing the alleged break in, we all decided that someone just wanted to scare us and cause a little excitement. It scared the crap out of me, and I am fearless!

Mrs. Varney

Mrs. Varney was an elderly lady that lived in the holler. She was a widow and had been for more years than I knew her. Henry Varney, her husband, was killed in the coal mine. She had two sons that were older than me. She may have had more children, but I don't know.

If she had shoes on, she might have been five feet tall, maybe 90 pounds soaking wet. Her skin was very brown and very wrinkly. I think she got it from working in the garden and her outside chores. She could chop wood like a man. She looked very frail and always wore a long dress. She might have been frail, but she didn't take s~t from anyone.

Her sons were grown men, and they were pretty husky. When she said to do this or that, there wasn't any, "I'll do it later" or "I'll do it tomorrow." It got done right then. When she spoke to them, they always answered, "Yes, ma'am."

In her living room, there was a large heating stove. It was big enough to heat the whole house. Beside the stove was a coal bucket, and across the room was her favorite chair. There was about 10–12 feet between the chair and the coal bucket.

She chewed tobacco all the time. I think her favorite brand was "Twist" or "Shoe Peg." These two brands were the strongest on the market.

When she was sitting in her favorite chair and chewing tobacco, she did not get up and go spit. She would lean forward, put two fingers up to her lips in the form of a V, and spit all the way across the room and hit the coal bucket every time. Sometimes when I was at her house, I would hang around waiting for her to miss the coal bucket, but she never did. She was a nice old lady. She would have made a good sniper in WWII.

Black Widow Spider

About ¼ mile down the road from where I lived was the Johnson family. The father was Troy, and he had a house full of kids. There were two about my age, and I played with them a lot. One daughter was named Nila, and one son was named Burley. All the other ones were younger than me, and I can't remember their names.

Near where they lived, someone had started to build a church. They had put up the basement walls. The floor may have been concrete, and there was always three to four inches of stagnant water standing in the basement. One wall had completely fallen in, and the other three were in different stages of collapsing. On the floor there were cinder blocks, boards, and many weeds growing on the floor and around the outside of the structure. Someone had good intentions long ago. It was a disaster now. All the kids played there. You could walk in the basement and step from cinder block to cinder block and not get your feet wet.

One day, we were all there playing, and Nila got bit by a black widow spider. Whether they took her to the hospital or not, I can't recall. I don't think they did. The hospital was 16 miles away and it cost money. She became very sick.

She was bed ridden for a long time. Even though she was able to get out of bed and move around, she was still sick for a long time. That was the last time any of us kids played at the old church. It was eventually filled in and leveled out. After a year or two, you couldn't tell anything had been there.

Ett's Spider

My mother's real name was Ethel, but just like everyone else, my sister and I called her Ett. I can't remember calling her "Mother" or "Mom"—only Ett. My dad always called her Ett when he was sober. When he was drunk, which was most of the time, he called her Ethel. As soon as he called her Ethel, my sister and I knew to stay out his way and make ourselves scarce.

My cousin, Karen, told me this story. One day, Ett and Karen were walking to the company store, probably for a pack of cigarettes.

There was a huge spider in the road. Karen said she didn't know if Ett just didn't see the spider or if she kicked it on purpose. Either way, when she did, hundreds of little spiders flew everywhere. I don't think she would have kicked it on purpose.

She didn't know if it was the big one or the smaller ones that bit her. The next day, she couldn't get out of bed. Her foot and leg swelled up so big, it looked like it was going to burst. She was in bed for two or three days. When she was able to get out of bed, she needed crutches for another week or two.

She should have gone to the doctor. Back then, you only went to the doctor if it was a life-or-death situation. Doctor visits cost money.

Baseball

In the early '50s, Patterson had a ragtag baseball team. It was made up mostly of men who worked at the mine, but anyone who could play ball was welcome. I had three uncles—Tom, Dick, and Harry. Don't laugh, it is the truth. That is what my Grandpaw and Grandmaw named them. All three played on the team at one time or another.

One Sunday, they were getting ready to go to a game. I decided I wanted to go too. When they left the house, I left with them. After about a mile down the road, they asked me, "Where are you going?" When they found out I was going with them to the game, they had a bunch of reasons why I shouldn't go. I kept walking with them. Harry broke down and offered me a quarter if I would go back home. I jumped on that quarter like a dog on a bone. He did not have to ask me twice. Back then, a quarter was a lot of money, especially for me. On my way back home, I had to pass a little mom-and-pop store. The store had bread, milk, and a few staples. They had a wide assortment of junk food, and I had a quarter, and the junk was calling my name. It wasn't long until I had a whole bag of candy, and Mrs. Limbach had my quarter. I ate the whole bag on the way home. That was the most candy I had ever eaten at one time. It didn't take too long for me to get sick. I think I must have OD'd on sugar.

This day wasn't going too good for me so far. No baseball game, no quarter, no candy, and sick to boot.

Getting back to the baseball team, there were two main reasons the men played ball. The first reason was to get away from the wives. The second reason was so they could drink a little "shine" and not have to listen to a ration of crap. The moonshine was the biggest reason they lost a few games.

On one particular Sunday, they had a game at Garden Creek. By the time they got there, most of them weren't feeling any pain. A few innings later, Claude Smith was pitching and my uncle, Dick, was the catcher. Garden Creek had a man on first base. Claude wound up and threw the ball. The man on first decided to steal second. The batter swung and missed. Uncle Dick had the ball in his mitt. He stepped out from behind the batter and threw the ball toward second to pick off the base runner. Claude turned around to watch the play at second base. "Whack!" Uncle Dick had hit Claude in the back of the head. Needless to say, the runner stole second with time to spare and went on to steal third base. I can't remember, but I think Garden Creek won.

There were a couple of players from Patterson that could have made the major league if they could have gotten out of the holler. Claude could throw a knuckle ball. From the time he released the ball till it got to the catcher's mitt, it did not spin. In addition, he could throw a drop ball, and the plate umpire would call it a strike. Then, the catcher would be digging it out of the dirt.

Claude had a son, Rayburn. He was a natural on the ball diamond. If he would have had someone to coach him and get him out of the holler, he would have made the major league.

Patterson had another game on one Sunday. I think it was at White-wood. They had a back stop. It was about 30 feet wide in front, about 12 feet high, and about 18 feet deep. Each ball team usually had one. Whitewood won the coin toss and would bat first. The umpire hollered, "Play ball!" The pitcher threw the ball as hard as he could. The ball went straight over the top of the back stop by at least five feet. It took a while to find the ball. The second pitch hit the left post that held the back stop up. The moonshine was working its magic. I think the pitcher was seeing double, which was the way most of the men played ball.

Most of the time up in the holler, us boys did not have a real baseball. Hillbilly ingenuity was a good thing. We would make one out of black tape. Usually, there was a good supply of tape because it was used a lot in the mine. We could find enough to make a ball. You start with nothing. Then, you stretch a long piece out and start rolling it up, around and around. Keep rolling it, and as you roll, try to keep it as round as possible. Keep rolling until you get it about as big as a baseball. The finished product is hard and heavy. A tape ball is better than no ball. Now, you'd be ready to hear the umpire yell, "Play ball!"

When you were at bat, you made sure you didn't get hit by a pitched ball. If you got hit, it would hurt like hell. It hurt more than a real baseball. When you were at bat, if you hit the ball a certain way, it would set your hands on fire. It only took two or three times at bat, and you learned how to hold the bat and hit the ball without setting your hands on fire. We also learned how to catch a ball with no glove. If you caught a line drive the wrong way, you knew it instantly. You would still know 15 minutes later.

Once in a great while, we would be lucky enough to get a real baseball. The real baseball was worth its weight in gold to us. If we were playing and the ball got away and was headed for the creek, you knew what you had to do to keep the ball from getting wet. Baseballs are made from cowhide, which is very tough. When we were lucky enough to get a real baseball, we proceeded to wear it out. Ah, those were the good old days!

Reunion and Dinner
on the Ground

Once a year, the Matney family had a reunion—a real big reunion. I did not think there were that many Matneys in the whole United States. Maybe they sent out flyers to all 48 states. I think they came out of the woodwork for the reunion. I am not a Matney, but I never missed one. I was invited, so I went. I can't remember when it was held or the name of the place.

Any kind of food you could think of was there and plenty of it. Those Matney ladies could sure stir it up. When they sat food on the table, you knew it was gonna be good. 99% of it was homemade—not just that "add water" store-bought crap.

Back then, I was a growing boy, and I could eat a bunch—a real *big* bunch. After a while, you could go back for more. I think I went with my buddy, Junior. If anything was happening in the holler that involved food, if we weren't there, then we were on our way.

You would have to go a long way to find a better party. The reunion lasted all day. I really enjoyed them and looked forward to the next year.

There were two churches in Patterson. One church was the Church of Christ. They would have dinner on the ground. The men of the church had the job of preparing a place to put the food. They would spread tablecloths on the ground. I think they were eating on the ground because, at certain points in the Bible, the Lord fed the people on the ground. After the church service, all the ladies prepared their best dishes and put them on the ground. It was a beehive of activity until everything was just right. After the pastor said the blessing, it was time to form the line.

Some of us boys had been waiting on this Sunday for three or four weeks. After the line had disappeared, we would just happen to walk by. Someone would ask us if we'd like to eat. You know they didn't have to ask us twice. Growing boys are always hungry. Everything was good and then better. These church ladies could cook! You didn't bring any store-bought crapola here. One of the ladies would make German chocolate cake that was out of this world. I always ate the desert first. If I waited too long, it would be gone. The next best thing was the pineapple upside-down cake. Next was the banana pudding. It was excellent also. We would help with the clean-up just in case they asked us if we wanted to take a plate home. When it came to food, we did not miss a trick.

Lantern & Chicken

My grandmaw always had a lantern. It had a special spot behind the cooking stove. Two or three times a year, she would send me down to the company store. I had a gallon jug in one hand and 10 cents in the other. If I was lucky, she would give me an extra nickel for a cold bottle of R.C. The extra nickel was a rare occasion.

That lantern was one of her prized possessions. Anytime she went anywhere at night, she always carried the trusty lantern. If it got moved from its spot behind the stove, it didn't take long until she missed it and told me about it. Wherever I had left it, I put it back where I found it as soon as possible. The lantern was older, but well maintained. I think it came over on the Mayflower. She always washed the glass after she used it. She kept the wick trimmed just perfect. I can't recall the lantern ever running out of kerosene.

Maw didn't put much faith in flashlights. They cost money. The batteries were expensive and did not last very long.

Occasionally when I brought in kindling to build a fire in the cook stove in the morning, she would douse a little bit of kerosene on it to help it get started. She only used a little bit of kerosene. Once in a while, she would sprinkle a little bit of sugar on the wood to help it get started.

Most of the time at night, we only had one light on in the house. Usually, we would sit in the kitchen and talk, do homework, or read. If we went into the living room, we would turn the light on in the living room and turn the light off in the kitchen. I don't recall how much the electric bill was or ever even seeing a bill. Maw always referred to electric as power. She would say, "Turn the power off."

We always had a nice Sunday dinner at 12:00 noon. 99.9% of the time, we always had some type of meat. It didn't make any difference what kind of meat or how much was on the table—you only got one piece. So, you better choose wisely. You got one piece of chicken, one pork chop, or one hamburger. Along with the meat, we had mashed potatoes, some type of gravy, and a vegetable. Our vegetable was anything from the garden that was ready to be picked. Some Sundays, she would bake a cake from scratch. Maw told me many times, "Don't make a pig out of yourself just because you can." When Monday rolled around, it was back to the basics of beans, potatoes, and cornbread.

I can't recall us ever having store-bought chicken. The Sundays that we had chicken, Maw or I would kill one. If Maw was going to kill it, she would sprinkle a little corn in the chicken house and all the chickens would come in to eat. Then, Maw would go in, shut the door behind her and take her pick. She would always have a wash tub waiting in the yard. Once she picked one out and caught it, she would go out in the yard. She would get ahold of the chicken's head in one hand and swing it around seven or eight times and give it a big jerk. Then, off came the chicken's head. She would put it under an upside-down tub. You could hear it flopping around for a couple of minutes. When it would quit flopping, she would pick up the tub. Then, she'd have a chicken ready to be cleaned. That process was called wringing its neck. Maw didn't think a thing about killing a chicken. She was a tough old girl.

If I was going to kill the Sunday dinner, Maw would point out the unlucky one that she wanted. I caught it exactly the same way that Maw did. Once I had it caught, I held it by its feet in my left hand and went to the chopping block where I cut wood. With the ax, I pushed the head down to the chopping block. If you push the head down real slow, it won't move. When the chicken is exactly where you want, then *whack*. Next, turn loose of the chicken and let it flop around for a minute or two. Now, it is ready to be cleaned. Cleaning the chicken is one of the worst jobs in the world. I have done it many times, and I hated every one of them. I won't go into the cleaning process at this time. I'll bet you are glad of that.

If it was a young chicken, then she would make Southern fried chicken. If it was an old hen or old rooster, she would make chicken and dumplings.

Television

Finally, TV came to Patterson, but not without a price. Buying a TV was just the first step.

The second step was to run a TV line from your new TV to the top of the mountain. That got to be work really quick. The TV line was two wires held apart by small pieces of plastic, which were about two inches and just a bit smaller than the diameter of a pencil. They were spaced about three inches apart. The best way to explain the line is, if you laid a piece down that was about a foot long, then it would look like a miniature railroad track.

To run the line up the mountain, you had to buy special hooks for the line to fit into. About every 50- or 60-foot span, you put a special hook into a tree. If you put the hooks too far apart, then the line would sag down. If the hooks were too close, then it cost a lot more money.

The third step was you had to buy an antenna. The antenna was installed in a really tall tree directly on top of the mountain. The antenna had to be installed in a really strong tree so that when a storm came by, it didn't damage the antenna. Now, hook the line to the antenna, and hopefully you can get television reception.

If a small twig or branch fell on the line, that killed the signal. Imagine you are watching your favorite football game, and the quarterback throws what might be the winning touchdown pass, and something falls on the line.

The television screen turns to snow, and you've got no sound. You'd jump up and start screaming, but for the wrong reason.

Then, you'd have to put your shoes and coat on if it is wintertime, climb all the way to the top of the mountain, taking off branches and twigs. Hopefully, a large limb didn't fall and break it. When you get back home, the football game has been over for two hours.

This was television in the mountains back then.

One of the miners asked Junior and me how much we would charge him to run his television line. Junior and I huddled and came up with a price of $2.50 or $5.00 total. We told him we would run it for $5.00.

The miner starts crying about the price. He tells us it isn't very far to his antenna and that there's probably nothing big on the line. It won't take us long. I thought to myself, *If it is that easy, then why does he need us?* He asks us if we would run it for $3.00 each. We ran the line for $6.00, and everyone was happy.

Hoot and Ethel Gibson bought a new television. It was a beautiful floor model. I think it was a Motorola.

When he got it home, he made a little mistake and asked us boys if we would help him get it in the house and help with the television line and antenna. We all pitched in.

After it was all set up and the antenna was adjusted just right, he had the best picture of any television in the whole holler. There were only three or four televisions at that time.

Every hillbilly who could find a place to watch wrestling would. Everyone knew each wrestler's name, all the stats about him, and who he was going to be wrestling next. It was a big deal.

If you wanted to start a fight, all you had to do was tell someone wrestling was all fake. As soon as you said "fake," if they didn't jump on you and beat you severely about the head and shoulders, you were lucky.

At that time, there were only three channels. If I remember right, the channels were 3, 5 and 8. At 12:00 a.m., all of the channels' signals signed off.

After they signed off, all you could see was black and white specks on the screen. It was called snow. Programming started again at 6 a.m.

All the programs were in black and white. Color television wasn't born yet.

Hoot asked us, "Would you like to come to my house and watch Saturday night wrestling?" It was like we just won season tickets on the 50-yard line.

Every Saturday night for a long time, we were front and center in front of Hoot's television. When we went in the house, we pulled our shoes off outside and sat in the floor.

I am sure after a few Saturday nights, this got old really quick for Hoot and Ethel. They never complained, and they treated us good. They had a good-looking daughter, and Hoot kept his eye on her.

Thank you, Hoot and Ethel. Rest in peace.

Love Letters

In the front of the company store, there were two doors. The door on the right went into the store. The door on the left was the post office and the main office of the Sycamore Coal Company. Gomer Evans and Hershel Miller worked there. The foyer was about 10 feet by 10 feet. Straight ahead was a wall with a little window with bars on it. There were a bunch of little boxes to the right of the window. The rest of the wall was covered with FBI wanted posters. If you wanted stamps, you had to go up to the little window and buy them. I bought many, many stamps there.

McKinley Matney delivered mail once a day to the post office. There were no mailboxes along the road. You had to go to the post office to get your mail. If you wanted to know if McKinley had delivered the mail that day, you would have to go up to the little window and ask, "Has the mail run yet?"

I had a friend, Gene Lawson, and he had a very pretty sister. His father worked at the mines in Patterson. Gene's mother had a sister, and her husband worked at a mine in Cinderella, West Virginia. The mine in Patterson and the mine in Cinderella were both owned by Sycamore Coal Company.

One weekend, Hassie's sister came over to Patterson for a weekend visit. I met the whole family. They had a nice-looking young daughter named Liz Ann. She and I got to be very good friends.

Anytime Gene and his family went over to Cinderella to visit, I made sure I went along. I got to see Liz Ann about once a month.

I would write her a letter and take it to the post office. Then, I went back to the post office every day to see if I had a letter from her. Postage stamps were three cents at the time. Pop bottles had a two-cent deposit on them. If I turned in two bottles to the company store, then I got four cents. That would equal one stamp and one cent toward the next one.

Many people in the hollow lost many pop bottles off their back porch because of that girl in Cinderella, West Virginia. There was one phone in the holler—not one phone per house. The coal company had the only phone in the whole holler. They guarded it like it was made of gold. If it was a life-or-death situation, you might get to use it for three minutes or less. If someone had been smart enough to put a pay phone in, they would have gotten rich. There wasn't another phone within a 10-mile radius.

Birthday Party

Every once in a while, maybe two or three times a year, someone in the holler would have a birthday party. This was one of the few ways the boys and girls would get together. Usually, we would get an invitation a couple of weeks in advance. This would give us plenty of time to get our Sunday best clothes washed and ironed. We all looked forward to these parties.

Anytime I went anywhere, my grandmaw made sure I had clean underwear on. "You just never knew when you might get into an accident and have to go to the hospital," she would say. All of us boys would wear our Sunday best, made sure our shoes were shined and that we did not step in any mud on the way to the party. We all slicked our hair down with Wild Root Cream Oil.

Elvis Presley was The King about this time. All the girls were in love. Elvis wore his hair in a D.A. or duck tail. We all tried to wear our hair the same way, but he looked much better than any one of us. Having money helped a great deal. Money does not talk; it stands up and screams.

Usually at the parties, there was cake, ice cream, bowls of potato chips, popcorn, Coke or Pepsi, and an assortment of junk food. Always, a record player was going, and a lot of the girls would dance—mostly with each other. Very few of the boys I ran around with knew how to dance. They thought it wasn't manly to dance. They thought it was sissified. I saw a real opportunity here. It didn't take me long to figure out that if you could dance, you could take your pick of the girls.

At the very next party, which was Peggy Lawson's birthday, her mother taught me how to dance. I probably stepped on her feet a dozen times. I'll give her credit—she didn't give up by the time the party was over. I think I had the basics down. I still had two left feet, but I was on my way. Thank you, Hassie, for being patient with me. She should have been wearing Fisty's hard-toe mining boots that night. It didn't take too long, and the girls were asking me to dance.

We played a game called spin the bottle. We all sat in the floor boy-girl, boy-girl all the way around. There was a pop bottle in the center of the circle on the floor. To start the game, one boy would give the bottle a big spin. If it stopped and was pointing at a boy, he would spin it again. If it stopped and was pointing to a girl, then the boy that spun the bottle and the girl would go into another room and kiss one time. Then, the girl would spin the bottle until it pointed at a boy, and they would go into another room and kiss. Usually, a daddy or mommy would watch and make sure no hanky panky took place. You have to remember this was in the '50s. Much has changed over the years. There was another game called Post Office, but I can't remember how it was played.

There wasn't any alcohol at these parties, and drugs were unheard of.

One of Edison Matney's kids had a birthday party. I can't recall which one. Anyway, the party had been going on for a while. Everyone was having fun. It was a nice party. About three or four of us boys were sitting on the edge of the bed, then one more sat down. When he sat down, the main frame rail of the bed broke, and that side of the bed hit the floor. It made a hell of a noise. That got everyone's attention. We just put too much weight on that side of the bed. I really felt sorry, but there wasn't anything anyone could do. We all told Edison we were sorry. I bet he felt like wringing our necks. We couldn't offer to pay for it. We didn't have one dollar between all of us. After the excitement died down, the party went on.

Edison helped me a lot over the years. He was a butcher by trade. Once, I was talking to him about becoming a butcher. He told me the very first lesson to becoming a butcher was to make damn sure you kept your left hand out of your right hand's way.

When Junior and I would be standing on the side of the road thumbing, Edison always stopped and picked us up. He never passed us up.

At the last Patterson reunion, I told him how much I appreciated all the rides and all the other ways he helped me.

Thank you again, Edison. Rest in peace.

Bath House

The coal mine had a building with about eight or 10 showers. There were no dividers or shower stalls—just showers along one wall. On the other side, there were lockers where the miners put their clean clothes in the top. In the bottom of the lockers, they put their mining clothes and boots.

There were about four or five burnside stoves lined up in the middle of the building. The stoves were spaced out evenly from end to end.

When the shift changed, the men going to work changed into their work clothes. The men that were finishing their shift would take a shower and change into their clean clothes and go home.

McKinley Matney ran the bath house. He delivered the mail to and from the Post Office. He also had a taxicab service. McKinley was a man who wore many hats.

McKinley gave all of us boys strict orders not to use the bath house. We would use up all the hot water and the miners would have to take a shower with cold water. Another thing was, if you didn't work for the coal company, you weren't allowed on company property. All of us boys knew what time the shift changed. All the men going to work came first. They changed their clothes and went up the hill to the mine so they would be ready to go in the mine when the man trip came out with all the men that were finishing up their shift. The men starting their shift would get in the coal cars to go inside the mine. The men finishing their shift would go down the hill to the bath house. The bath house was a mad house for about one hour. After that, there wasn't anyone taking a shower for about seven hours.

McKinley would come down to the bath house later in the evening. He would sweep up the floor and pick up all the paper and clean up the mess the miners left. He would fix the fires and put a lot of coal in each stove so it would last till the next morning. He took good care of everything. Once he left for the night, we knew he wouldn't be back till the next morning.

All of us boys that wanted to take a shower would wait till after dark. Then, we would slip over there. One winter night, we were at the bath house to take a shower. The stoves were hot and, inside the bath house, the temperature was a little chilly.

You always put newspapers down to stand on after the shower so you wouldn't get your feet dirty, and it kept you from getting athlete's foot. In the winter, you put the papers down near the stove so you could stay warm while you dried off. We all had our papers down near the stoves.

We were having a good time. As soon as we got done showering, we ran over near a stove and stood on the papers to dry off.

When we were there, we were always in a hurry to get a shower and get out of there. We didn't want to get caught by one the miners who might tell on us or get caught by McKinley.

One of the boys was standing by the stove, drying himself off as quickly as he could. Well, he bent over to dry his feet. When he did that, he touched the stove with his butt. No one had to tell him to move. He scorched his rear pretty good. He couldn't sit down for a while. The stove's name is Burnside. Now you know how it got its name.

I think McKinley knew we were taking showers. I don't really think he cared. Once he told us not to take showers or be on company property. He told us this so if we got hurt or anything happened, his ass would be covered.

McKinley brought the mail up to the Post Office about the same time each day. If we were walking and needed a ride, we would be sure to be on the road about the time for him to come by. We could hear him coming about five minutes before he got there. We knew the sound his car made. He couldn't resist stopping and asking if you needed a ride. He never charged us anything. He knew you can't get blood out of a turnip. When my mother needed a ride to Grundy or any place, she would ask McKinley, and he never said no. Also, only very seldom did he ever charge her for a ride. If he did charge her, it was only about half of what it should have been. I don't know how he made any money with his taxi.

McKinley had a brother named Morgan. He and my mother spent a lot of time at the same hospital. McKinley is high on my list of good men. I wish I could thank him for all the free rides and all of the showers that he provided me and the rest of the boys in Patterson. Thanks again.

Coal Mining & No Money

In Patterson, most of the men worked at the Sycamore Coal Company or jobs related to the mine. A few of the men had jobs in Grundy or surrounding areas. The coal mine was the main source of income.

When the economy was good, the mines worked five to six days a week. All the miners had money in their pockets. But when the economy slowed down, the mines slowed down too. Some weeks, the mine would only work two or three days a week. Some weeks were zero days. No one had an extra penny in their pocket. Most of the miners lived in company houses. They bought 90% of their provisions and gas from the company store. Most of the time, they charged everything. If you had a big family, after a couple of weeks, your bill was high. The store had just about everything you would need. It had groceries, meats, dried goods, shoes, and boots. They had a drum of kerosene inside and a gas pump outside.

The miners were paid every half, usually on the 1st and 15th of the month. After your grocery bill, gas bill, rent and any advances you owed for were deducted from your pay, there wasn't much left, especially if you were only working two or three days a week. Occasionally, someone would get an advance on their check. Likely, after they got their payday, some of the miners would receive zero pay and still owe the company money.

New Bike

Dougie Mays lived up in the hollow, not far from where I lived. He was a couple of years older and a couple of grades ahead of me in school. I think he was in the same grade as my sister, Sue.

There was brand of notebook paper called Lucky Star. It was probably the only brand available to us at that time. There were about 20 sheets of paper per pack. It was five cents. A pack of paper had a yellow band around it with a big star in the middle. The bands were kind of like what the banks used around packs of money.

If you saved these lucky stars, you could get a prize. The more you saved, the bigger the prize.

Dougie saved every one he could; he didn't let one get by him. Most all the other kids saved their stars for Dougie. Over a four-year period, he saved 1,500 Lucky Stars. Four years is a long time, and 1,500 is a hell of a lot of Lucky Stars.

He sent them off to the paper company. After a few weeks, which probably seemed like an eternity to him, he picked up the bike at the railroad freight station in Grundy. It was the prettiest bike I had ever seen. It was beautiful.

I can't remember ever seeing another new bike up in the holler. There were a few old traps in the holler. I had one. I don't remember how I managed to get it. Two things are for sure. I didn't steal it, and I didn't buy it with cash. Cash money was hard to come by.

In the holler, when you are riding your bike and come to an incline, you stand up and ride so you can put more pressure on the pedal. As the road gets steeper you put more pressure on the pedal. When the road gets real steep, you pull up on the handlebars and push down on the pedal as hard as you can.

I was on the old mining road, and some places are very steep. Trying to make it to the top, I was pulling up on the handlebars and pushing down as hard as I could. Bang! The pedal broke off the crank. The crossbars on the bicycle stopped my fall. One small problem, though, was that my "package" hit the crossbar first. That was the hardest I had ever been hit there. It made me sick instantly. Everything swelled up and up and up for about a week. I don't have any children and no suspects. I wonder why.

Uncle Billy

Everyone called him Uncle Billy. Uncle Billy Matney was an icon up in the holler. For as long as I can remember, there were always a lot of Matneys in the holler. I think he might have been the oldest one of the Matney clan. Everyone for miles and miles around knew him, and probably everyone in Buchanan County knew him.

The first time I saw him, he was an old man. The last time I saw him years and years later, he hadn't changed one bit. He looked exactly the same. He was rather thin and walked kind of bent over. He wore an old hat, and he always had a pipe in his mouth. I don't remember ever seeing him light it or any smoke coming out of it. I do remember seeing spit drip off the end.

He had a huge farm on top of the mountain. Probably the easiest way to get to his farm was to go straight up Horn Holler and follow the road all the way to his gate where the sign says no trespassing.

We lived at the mouth of Horn Holler. Every time Uncle Billy went up to his farm or came down, he had to pass our house. He came by three or four times a week.

My grandpaw passed away years and years ago, so Maw was a widow. Uncle Billy was a widower. Every time I saw Uncle Billy coming up or down the road, I would run and tell Maw her boyfriend was coming. She didn't think that it was funny at all.

I think his farm had quite a few acres. Right on top of the mountain was his house. It was a two-story log house. No paint—just weathered logs. I was never inside, but I am sure it was nice in its day. There was also a huge barn. It was made from logs and a few boards.

Uncle Bill had one son, John D. He might have had other children... I don't know. Uncle Billy couldn't deny John D. He was a younger version of Uncle Billy. He stood at least 6'2" or more. He didn't have one ounce of fat anywhere. He had the same walk as his dad, except with a little more spring in his step. If you saw John D. coming a mile away, you knew who it was by the way he walked.

Early one spring, John D. got the bright idea that he was going to do a little farming on the mountain. He was going to grow green beans.

He plowed about a two-foot-wide furrow about 200 feet long, maybe a little farther. Then, a step up the hill maybe two or three feet, he plowed another furrow. The idea behind leaving a two- or three-foot-wide strip of land not plowed was so the green beans could run up the weeds as they grew. I don't know how many acres he planted. It was a whole field, and it was all fenced in with split rails.

Everything was going great. The beans were planted. There was plenty of rain and plenty of sun. The ground was very good. Finally, it came harvest time. He had a bumper crop. Green beans were everywhere.

They were growing faster than he could get them picked. He had green beans coming out of his ying yang. He hired all of us boys to help pick and anyone else he could con into picking. I think it paid maybe 50 cents a bushel. It takes a lot of beans to fill a bushel basket when you are hot in the sun and bent over picking. John D. had a mule and sled to haul the beans off the mountain. The old mule had its work cut out for it. I picked all day out in the hot sun with no shirt on. That night, my back was covered with about a million little blisters. It is a miracle I didn't have a sun or heat stroke. I think I had second degree burns.

Sunscreen probably wasn't available at that time. The company store wouldn't have had any. It is just as well no one had any money to buy any. I don't remember how many bushels I picked or how much money I made. Whatever the amount, it wasn't worth it. One day on the mountain and picking beans was enough for me.

John D. hauled beans off the mountain from daylight till dark. I hope he made a lot of money. If he didn't, it wasn't because he didn't work at it.

That was the first year and last year. The Green Bean King tried his hand at green bean farming.

Here is one of the hillbilly ways of preserving green beans:

1. Take all the strings off the beans.
2. Get a large needle and a long piece of good string.
3. Take each bean one at a time and run the needle through the center of the bean.
4. After you have strung a good amount, tie each end of the string together. It should look like a giant green bean necklace.
5. Hang them up in a dry place and forget about them till the middle of the winter.

To cook them, do the following:

1. Take the beans off the string.
2. Put them in a large pot, and make sure all the beans are under water.
3. Let them soak overnight.
4. After the soaking, drain the water off and put about half as much water back in the pot.
5. Put a piece of salt pork in the pot.
6. Cook down about 3 hours or until done.

Enjoy! They are delicious. The hillbilly's name for the beans is leather britches. When my grandmaw strung the beans, she would hang them behind the cooking stove in the kitchen. My grandmaw "did so much with so little for so long she could take nothing and do anything." When you don't have anything, you can make do.

She told me several times, "Don't ever throw anything away that somebody or something can eat."

Mirror

I stayed a lot with my Uncle Dick. He lived in Vansant on the side of the river. One of my favorite things to do was go up and down the riverbank to look for treasures. One day I found a mirror about three feet in diameter. It amazed me that it wasn't broken. That was a real find. When I left his house, I took the mirror up to Patterson to Maw's house. You just can't tell when you might need a good mirror.

Maw always had a few chickens. She would get a steady supply of eggs, and when the little ones grew up, each one was a Sunday chicken dinner. At this time, she had about six or eight hens and one rooster. The rooster thought he was the king of the hill. He hadn't met the mirror yet. I sat the mirror up and leaned it back against the house. Then, I sprinkled a little corn in front of the mirror. It took maybe an hour before the hens found the corn. They started picking and eating. Pretty soon the rooster came around in front of the mirror. As soon as he saw the rooster in the mirror, the fight was on. The rooster was fighting as hard as he could. The rooster in the mirror was fighting back lick for lick. Neither one was giving up. The rooster would back off a couple of feet, then he would hit the rooster in the mirror again. The fight had been going on for a few minutes. This was better than wrestling on Saturday night television. I was having a lot of fun.

Pretty soon, here comes the referee with her broom. Maw runs the rooster off and makes me put the mirror away. It was a good fight while it lasted. I put the mirror up in the smoke house.

Some day when Maw isn't looking, I'll get the mirror out and we will have round two.

I guess by now you have figured out there wasn't much entertainment in the hollow. We had to make our own. We never got around to round two. I sold the mirror for three dollars and made out like a bandit.

Maw's rooster was still king of the hill.

Go-Cart

One of my jobs was to make sure we had plenty of coal. I would go to the slate dump and pick up a couple of buckets of coal and carry it home. It didn't take long before this got to be real work. There had to be a better way. I put out an A.P.B. for four wagon wheels and two axles. I don't remember where they came from. The main thing was I got them.

I built a homemade wagon. It wouldn't win a beauty contest. It was pretty crude, but it worked. About a mile up the road was an old Number 3 washtub in the creek. After I got the tub home and nailed it to the wagon, carrying coal was history. It saved me a great deal of work.

My Uncle Tom bought us a gas-powered reel type lawnmower. Where he got it and how much he paid is anybody's guess. It worked well, and I kept the grass and weeds mowed.

One day a week for mowing the grass, and six days a week it sat under the house gathering dust. I took the motor off the mower and the tub off the wagon and married the motor and wagon together. It took a little hillbilly ingenuity and a lot of trial and error. Once the bugs got worked out, it worked great.

I would ride it down to the company store and get Maw's provisions and ride it back home. There was only one slight problem: no brakes. When you wanted to stop, you'd just have to shut the engine off. The compression in the engine worked exactly like a jake brake works on large trucks. It slowed you down. Then, you would come to a stop.

It would go very fast, much faster than walking. It was a lot of fun while it lasted. But we all know all good things come to an end sooner or later.

It wasn't long before my Uncle Tom found out about it. When something happened up in the holler, it didn't take long for the news to spread. Tom came over and gave me little talking to.

I had to reverse the process by taking the mower motor off the wagon and put it back on the mower where I found it. Then, I put the Number 3 washtub back on the wagon.

I don't know when go-carts were born. I might have had one of the first homemade go-carts to hit the road. I wish I had a picture or two of that low-mileage jewel.

Hog Slaughter

If you have a weak stomach, you might want to skip this chapter. This chapter goes back a long way in the history of hillbillies and what they did to survive. My role wasn't very big in this process. I was there a few times.

Occasionally, someone up in the holler would slaughter a hog. This always happened in the fall when it was cool. The first step was to build a place to sit two large washtubs over a fire. A few choice rocks were placed wide enough to have a fire, but just far enough that the tubs sat on them over the fire.

The tubs were filled with water and heated until it was boiling. The water had to be scalding hot and plenty of it. Once the process started, they couldn't run out. They also needed a bunch of burlap feed sacks, some sharp knives, one real long one, and usually a sheet of plywood to lay the hog on.

If the water is boiling and everything is ready, someone shoots the hog between the eyes. The hog drops instantly. Someone cuts about a three-inch gash across the front of its chest, all the while the hog is kicking frantically. Then, they take the long knife and stick it in the cut as far as it will go, up to the handle. When the knife is withdrawn, blood starts pumping out of the cut with each heartbeat. Gradually, the blood stops and the hog stops kicking. Now, it is time to go to work.

The hog was laid on the plywood and covered with burlap feed sacks. Scalding water was poured on the feed sacks, and a lot of it.

Now, it was time for me to go to work, filling the tubs back up with water and putting more wood on the fire. It took quite a bit of wood to keep the water boiling. After the sacks had been on the hog for a few minutes, it was completely scalded. The feed sacks were taken off. Two or three men would start scraping the side of the hog that had been scalded. Once they had it scraped from head to tail, they would turn it over on its side and start the process all over again. It always amazed me how clean it was after it had been scraped. It was perfectly clean after both sides were scraped. It was time to hang it up.

A slit was cut on its hind legs between the tendon and the bone near the hoof. They had a 4" by 4", about three feet long, and sharpened on both ends. Each end was inserted in the slit on the hind legs. They used this to hang the hog up with. The first thing they cut off was its head.

Then, it was split from its boongie to its neck, and all the insides were taken out. They saved a few pieces—heart and liver. I think that was all, but I am not sure. Once the cavity was thoroughly cleaned, they proceeded to cut it up. I would help clean up the mess. My pay was a piece of meat. Now you know how to slaughter a hog.

Molasses

Once a year, late in the fall, one of the families up in the head of the holler would make molasses.

They would grow sugar cane all summer long. It was planted in early spring and harvested in the late fall. In the fall, the cane is cut, and the stalks are run through a press. This gets all the juices out of the cane.

A boiling pan about three feet wide, five feet long, and maybe five or six inches deep was used. The pan sat on some rocks and a fire was built under the pan. The cane juice came to a boil. While it was boiling, it was constantly stirred back and forth until the juice was cooked down and got very thick.

Once it got very thick and stiff, it was done. My job was to keep the fire going from start to finish. My pay for tending the fire was one quart of molasses.

While all this was happening, a half-gallon jug of moonshine was sitting by the drinking water bucket. You could drink all you wanted of either one.

This was more of a social gathering and party than work.

If you haven't chewed on a raw cane stalk and you get the chance, don't pass it up. And if you get the chance, drink some raw cane juice. It is really good.

Fidel Castro's favorite drink was sugar cane juice and Cuban rum. If you get the chance to go to Cuba, go.

Shooting Rabbit

J ake Smith was a tall, raw-boned mountain man from the word go. What was his was his, and what was yours was yours. There wasn't any gray area. He always had a nice garden and a small apple orchard.

He had a large house with a wraparound front porch. The house sat on the side of the mountain. The back of the house was at ground level, and the front of the house was quite a few feet off the ground. If you sat on his front porch, you could see up and down the holler. His house sat quite a way up the side of the mountain from the main road. He owned some land farther up the mountain. On that piece of land was a spring, and he piped the water to his house. His house was probably the first house with running water in the whole hollow.

One day, he hollered at me and motioned for me to come down to his house. When I got there, he was sitting on the front porch. His .22 rifle was there leaning on the handrail. He asked me if I would run an errand for him. Naturally, I said yes. He pointed across the holler. The pastor of the Church of God lived over there. In the pastor's garden, he said he shot a rabbit and wanted me to go get it.

From his house, I went down the hill, across the road, across the creek, across the railroad, up the other side of the holler and to the garden. I could see him on his porch flailing his arms wanting me to move up the hill. Up the hill and in the lettuce bed, there was the rabbit.

I think it is about the length of two football fields from his porch across the holler to the garden. I don't remember the .22 rifle having a scope on it.

I am sure Mr. Smith and his wife had rabbit for supper. 99% of the hunters in the holler carried a shotgun in the woods. Mr. Smith always carried his trusty .22. He would have made a good sniper in the army. Their motto is one shot, one kill.

Sleigh Ride

In Virginia, you don't get very many big snows—not enough for us boys. But when we did, we made the most of it. We welcomed it with open arms. When it did come, we always listened to the radio to see if school had been cancelled. If school was cancelled for any reason, we had to make it up at the end of the school year. The make-up time was a long way away. The snow was *now*, and we took advantage of it. When the roads get snow-covered in the mountains, they get very slick and dangerous. Back then, there were not any snowplows—not up in Patterson anyway. The bridges were usually the first to get snow-covered and slick. You had to be very careful on them.

If we didn't have to go to school the next day, then we didn't have to go to bed early. We could sleigh ride as long as we wanted. Our favorite place to sleigh ride was the road that goes up to the mine. It has a bunch of curves and is plenty steep from top to bottom. At the bottom was the tipple, and there was a cinder block building about 14' x 14'. Inside was a coal stove in the center, and there were benches against the wall on three sides. This building was used for the miners waiting on a ride up the hill. The miners kept a good supply of coal for the stove. There were a few other buildings scattered here and there, but this one worked great for us.

We would get a roaring fire going in the bottom one-third of the stove. It would glow red hot. If there was any snow on top of the building, it didn't take long for it to start melting. This was our staging area for a night of sleigh riding.

From the little building up to the top of the mountain, there is a short-cut the miners took it they wanted to walk up the mountain to the drift mouth of the mines to go to work.

This shortcut started at the little building we were using. The path went by the tipple up a little way past the bath house and on up the hill through a patch of pawpaw trees, then past the water storage tank to the bath house. This tank was maybe 10' x 10' and about eight feet deep. After you pass the tank, you continued up the hill maybe 500 more feet, and you are at the top of the mine road. From the bottom to the top was about a 15-minute walk. Near the drift mouth was two or three buildings. One smaller one was the lighthouse. This is where the miners got their light and battery. The light snapped on the miner's hardhat. An electric cord went from the light to the battery. The battery hooked to the miner's belt. He was ready to go in the mines. Near the drift mouth was a larger building; this is where repairs were made on most of the equipment.

My Uncle Tom worked there, he was an electrician and mechanic. This area was wide and level. About 300 feet from there, the road started and it started down immediately. This was where we started our sleigh ride to the bottom. It was about ¾ mile of fun and excitement.

We would hold the sleigh and take off running. When we were running as fast as we could, in one motion we would hit the ground with the sleigh and hit the sleigh with our body lying on the sleigh our head was to the front and our feet sticking out the back. We started picking up speed instantly.

You couldn't sit up on the sleigh, as fast as we would go. There is no way you could hold on and make the curves. If you missed a curve and went over the side of the mountain, your next ride would be in a long black Cadillac with slow walking and sad singing.

No one ever missed a curve. It only took a couple hundred feet, and you were at breakneck speed. The first curve came up fast, and by the second curve you were going so fast you had to drag your feet.

The ride was just getting started. The further, the faster. By now, your eyes were watering so bad it looked like you were crying. The tears would freeze in your eye lashes.

Near the end of the ride was about a 1,000-foot straight stretch at about a 15% decline. When you got to the bottom, you didn't need wings. You were flying.

When you coasted to a stop, you were within one hundred feet of the little building where you could get warm and get your nerve up to do it again.

Those were some of the best days of my life. I just didn't know it at the time. Money can't buy these memories.

No Money

One of the miners wanted to put a root cellar under his house. He asked me if I wanted to help him. I jumped on the job like a chicken on a June bug. I forgot to talk about the most important thing—money. Big mistake on my part.

We started working on it every evening for about two or three hours. It was hard work. It was going to be about 10 feet wide and straight back into the hillside. It was hard digging because you didn't have any room to swing a pick. When we shoveled a little dirt into a wheelbarrow, we would take it out and dump it over the hill. I would go home dirty and tired.

This went on for about a week. Maw asked if he paid me. I told her no, but at the end of every day, he always said, "Thank you." She didn't want to hear this. She had to wash my dirty clothes. Soap and electricity cost money.

She told me in no uncertain terms that the next time he says, "Thank you," you tell him you can't put thank you in your pocket and hold out your hand.

It worked great from then on. He paid me every evening and paid me for the days he missed, too.

I learned a valuable lesson from that experience. Make sure you settle on a price before the work starts.

Haircut

My best friend and the boy I ran around with was Junior Matney. He and I got into and out of a lot of stuff. He had an older brother, Larry, and two or three younger brothers. I was at their house a great deal. His mom probably got tired of seeing me. About every month or six weeks, his dad, Henry, would cut all the boys' hair. Junior would let me know when this was going to happen. I would make sure I was front and center when Henry brought out the clippers and sheet. After he cut Junior and Larry's hair most of the time, he would ask me if I wanted a haircut. Naturally, I would say yes. Henry was a good barber. He didn't give a soup bowl haircut.

When you are broke and don't have any money, sometimes you have to swallow your pride and take a handout. Whenever he finished cutting his boys' hair and didn't ask me, I would ask him if he had time to cut my hair. He said yes and cut it. I don't think he cared if he cut one more.

If I missed the haircutting appointment, I would have to wait until the next appointment. If I missed the next one, I would look like a shepherd dog and need dog tags. I could have gotten a haircut in Grundy, but they cost 50 cents or a dollar. That is a lot of money to a poor boy like me. Thank you, Henry.

One time, Henry went fishing and took his crew. I think they went to South Holston Lake. He asked me to go with them, and that was nice of him to take me. Thanks for the fishing trip. It was great.

Flood of '57

In 1957, there was a flood in Buchanan County to end all floods. It was a disaster for the whole county. Many people lost all their possessions. Also, a lot of houses and house trailers went down the river.

I was staying at my Uncle Dick and Aunt Betty's house at that time. They lived in the first house down the river from the big Vansant Elementary School.

The school sat on the edge of the riverbank. My uncle's house was on the edge of the river too.

At first it started raining slowly, then it kept getting harder and harder. Then, the river behind Uncle Dick's house started rising slowly but surely. It was coming up.

Uncle Dick had a coal truck at the time. We took the tailgate off the truck, then backed it up to the back porch. The river was up to the backyard and showing no signs of slowing down.

We loaded all the furniture that was in the house into the truck. The dressers still had clothes in them. Some of the dishes were dirty. The water was up to the porch now. There is only a 6" step from the porch to the house floor.

When we were loading the last piece of furniture, the water was starting to come into the house. The wheels on the truck were ¾ of the way underwater. It was definitely time to go to higher ground.

When we were loading the truck, we could see everything floating down the river. My Uncle Dick started to get a little nervous when we saw a medium-sized house trailer with about a half a dozen chickens on the roof floating down the river. Old tires, hundreds of logs, outhouses, oil drums, and anything that could float did.

After a couple of days, the water started to go down and we went back to the house. The water came up about two feet inside the house. The yard was a total mess.

We cleaned all the mud out of the house and, after a day or two, it dried out and we moved the furniture back in.

The elementary school took the brunt of the water. About ¼ of the back wall was gone. My uncle told me if the school hadn't been there, then his house would have been gone.

One man up the river tied his house to a large tree. The house floated off the foundation. It only went to the end of the rope.

One of the bridges in Grundy had a house trailer wrapped around one of its columns and tons of other stuff on all the other columns. A little bit more, and the bridge would have been gone.

The town of Grundy was a mess, a lot of the businesses lost a great deal of merchandise.

There was a Ford dealership and many of their cars were completely underwater. Some had only minor water damage. They couldn't sell them as new, so they sold them cheap. My Uncle Tom bought a green and white Ford four-door V-8 standard shift. After they cleaned it up, it looked brand new. There were no signs of water damage. He drove that car for years and years and never had one minute's trouble out of it.

New House

My Uncle Tom and Aunt Ocie had two daughters, Brenda and Kathy. They lived in the holler in a company house. He was an electrician and mechanic at the mine. When the miners were working five or six days, some of the miners would work a lot of overtime. If something broke down and that piece of equipment was needed to produce coal, my Uncle Tom was one of the men that repaired it. If his eight-hour shift was over and the piece of equipment wasn't fixed, then he would work overtime. This was called doubling back. He would work his usual eight hours, then double back for eight more hours. The second eight hours paid time and one half. If it was on Sunday or a holiday, it paid double time. Most of the time when something broke down, it was inside the mine and at the face. The face is where the digging of the coal takes place. When the mines were working five and six days a week, all the miners made good money.

This made up for some of the lean times, and there were many of them. I overheard one of the miners talking to someone, and he said, "Some weeks, you eat the chicken, and some weeks, you eat the feathers." I guess that just about told it like it was.

Tom and Ocie saved their money and bought a house in Richlands, Virginia. It was a nice house—not right in the downtown area, but still in the city limits. There was an abundance of wildlife around their house.

Squirrels, rabbits, coons, opossums, snakes, and an assortment of other critters were near the house. Before they moved in, they did a major house cleaning and painting. Every room was painted whether it needed it or not. If it didn't move, it got painted. Tom bought many gallons of paint and a sack full of brushes and rollers. Tom must have really liked me because he gave me the job of being a jack of all trades. I was the janitor, and I dusted, mopped, prepped for the painting man, painted, did yard maintenance, and anything else that needed to be done. I painted more on that house than I had painted in my entire life. I painted, cleaned, carried out trash, did yard work. This was a major operation. I wore many hats on that job. I must admit that when we got done, it looked like a new house. I don't remember helping them move in, but maybe I did. I do remember being glad when it finally happened.

They had been living in the new house for a while. Ocie was doing the wash, and she noticed something hanging on her clothes basket. It wasn't your usual rag or piece of string you would suspect. It was a snakeskin, a big snakeskin. When a snake sheds it skin, it will start to shed, and a little piece will hang up on something. The snake kept on going. Eventually the snake left its whole skin hanging somewhere, like on the side of a clothes basket.

My Uncle Tom didn't like snakes at all. Tom and Ocie tore the house apart, pulling all the cushions off the couch and turning it upside down and taking all the bed clothes off. They looked any place you could think of. No snake. Tom filled every crack and crevice he thought a snake could crawl through. He spent a small fortune on caulk and crack filler. They didn't find the snake, but they did manage to kill a small one in the front yard.

Girlfriend's Marriage

When I was in maybe the 11th grade in high school, I had my eye on this one girl. She had really long black hair and blue eyes. Many of the boys had their eye on her, too.

I finally worked up the courage to talk to her. After just a few minutes, I knew we were going to get along good. She was very easy to talk to. She talked 90 mph. All I had to do was listen and answer occasionally.

When my bus unloaded at the high school, I went straight to where her locker was. If she wasn't there, her bus hadn't arrived yet. I would go out in the lot and wait for her. She rode the bus that went up Slate Creek. We would walk the halls and talk until classes started.

Some of her classes were near my classes. During class change, I would get to see her for a few minutes. When school let out in the evening, I would walk her to her bus. This went on for a couple of months.

One morning, I met her bus in the lot. All the kids get off, but not her. I asked some of her friends about her, but no one knew where she was. The next morning, one of her friends gave me a note from her. She was sick and going to miss school for a while. I missed her a great deal. We passed notes back and forth. No cell phone back then.

She sent me one note and said she wanted me to come and see her. It was about 15 miles as the crow flies from my house to her house. She lived all the way up to the head of Slate Creek on Bradshaw Mountain. I decided when Saturday rolled around, I would go see her. Saturday came, and I took off early from my house. I walked to the head of the holler, crossed the top of the mountain down the other side, and came out at Slate Creek Post Office. When I got to the post office, I headed up Slate Creek. My plan was to hitchhike to her house. It was maybe eight or nine miles more. It is called hitchhiking for a good reason. Sometimes this mode of transportation is called thumbing. When a car goes by, you stick your thumb out and hope they will stop and give you a ride.

After about two or three hours, I finally came to the road that she lived on. Another half of a mile and I would be there. I began to come to the conclusion that this wasn't such a hot idea. But hillbillies are a stubborn breed, and I had too much invested to turn back now.

Finally, I get to her house. The big moment had arrived, so I pecked on the door and her mother answered. She invited me in. My sweetheart was in the living room laying on the couch with a blanket on her. She kind of turned on her side and motioned for me to sit on the couch with her.

I had been there for about an hour when her daddy came in. I stood up, and she introduced me to him, and we shook hands. There wasn't any doubt that he was about two-thirds drunk. He and I talked for a few minutes. Then, her brother came in, and I stood up and shook his hand. Her daddy introduced me by saying, "This is John. He is my next son-in-law."

My ears perked up when he said that. It didn't take me long to see the light, and it pointed toward Patterson and home. I stayed for about another half hour and got my a- - outta there. ASAP.

I hitchhiked off the mountain. Here is the icing on the cake. One car came along, and I stuck my thumb out. The car stopped about 100 feet past me. I was running toward the car. Some guy hung his head out of the passenger side and hollered, "I caught this one! You can catch the next one!" Then, they sped off. I am sure they got a big laugh out of it. A-holes.

When I got to the Slate Creek Post Office, I turned left and walked back across the mountain.

That was the first and last time I was in her house. The girl was very pretty, but not that pretty. This boy wasn't ready to even think about marriage. No more trips up Slate Creek for me. One was plenty. I am sure she made some lucky guy a beautiful wife.

One other young lady caught my eye. She was very pretty, also. She was one year ahead of me in school. Some lucky guy wanted everyone to know she was already spoken for. The diamond ring on her finger did not come out of a Cracker Jack box. Her fiancé worked some place in Kentucky. He must have had a good-paying job. The ring she had on wasn't cheap.

I knew she was engaged, but that didn't stop me. She wasn't married yet. If she wasn't interested, she wouldn't have given me the time of day. I would talk to her in the hall and walk her to her first class. I would carry her books to the bus every evening. She always had a lot of books. She would wear a blue pullover sweater and a black skirt. She made the sweater and skirt look good.

One day, I carried her books to her bus. Before we got to the bus, I saw a strange man standing by the door, and it wasn't the driver. When we got there, she introduced me to him. It was her future husband. Oh s--t! I handed her the books, said good-bye, and vanished into the crowd.

I was hoping I didn't get her in any trouble. She didn't need any trouble.

The next morning, I was waiting for her to get off the bus. When she got off, she was all smiles. I told her I was worried I might have gotten her in trouble. She said not to worry and that everything was okay. I carried her books as if nothing had happened and continued till the end of the school year.

That year, she graduated, and it was all over. I would have liked to have seen her again, but there was no way. I had no car, no job, and no money. I couldn't afford the box the engagement ring came in. She had a bright future. She had a young brother that was a year or two behind me in school. He kept me up to date on what was happening in her life. She did marry that guy.

Writing on the Roof

When my grandfather was living, he worked for the mines there in Patterson. He was a mechanic and an electrician, I think. When he passed away in 1946, he left behind my grandmother and five kids at home. There wasn't any welfare system or food stamps. Back then, I am sure it was very hard.

At that time, the mines took care of their employees. The house where Grandpaw and Maw lived belonged to the coal company, and they paid rent just like all the rest of the miners.

Maw had almost no income, so it was hard for her to come up with the rent money.

The company sold her a house for almost nothing and gave her a lifetime lease for one dollar a year on the land. She had to keep the repairs and maintenance upon the house as long as she lived there.

As I got older, it got to be my job to take care of all the small repairs. One summer, it came a bad storm with a lot of wind and rain. The wind ripped a small piece of tar paper off the roof, and we got a small leak in the living room. It was my job to get up there and fix the leak. I had a gallon of tar that turned almost silver when it dried good.

Patching the roof wasn't a big deal—maybe two hours at the most. The patch looked almost professional.

I had a sweetheart at that time. She was a cute little thing. She and I got along really good.

I decided to put mine and her initials on the roof in the front of the house so that when the tar dried, everyone could see the initials when they drove by the house. The next morning, I couldn't wait to see the artwork on the roof. So, I went out in the road and looked back. Sure, enough you could see our initials. The artwork was perfect in my eyes. At a certain time of day when the sun was just right, they would shine almost like chrome. When my girlfriend saw the artwork, she knew beyond a shadow of a doubt I really liked her.

Everything was good for a month or two. Maw would go out and pick up trash every now and then. One day, she went out to the far side of the road to pick up some trash, and on her way back, she saw the artwork on the roof.

Maw hollered for me to come out there. I could tell by the tone of her voice she meant business. She pointed to the roof. I saw the writing on the roof and the writing on the wall at the same time.

About 15 minutes later I was on the roof with the tar bucket painting over my beautiful artwork.

The new paint job didn't go unnoticed. Several people asked me, "Did you break up with your girlfriend?" We were still a couple for a while, but eventually we did break up. I think she let a good one get away. She probably thinks I let a good one get away.

Blackie

My Uncle Dick lived in Vansant on the side of the Levisa River near the Vansant Elementary school. He and his wife, Betty, had four little kids. They looked like stair steps. The oldest was Penny Sue, next was Dickie Gene, and then Buzzy and Judy.

One day, a stray dog came to Dick's house and took up residency. I think the kids were getting food out of the refrigerator and feeding it. Dick and Betty didn't want the dog. They didn't want the kids getting attached to it. He brought the dog up in the holler and gave it to Maw and me. Maw couldn't turn any stray away. The dog found a home that day.

It was solid black except for a little patch of white on its chest. He didn't have a name, so we named him Blackie. He turned out to be a great dog. He was a good watchdog. I should have named him Timex. We had a small problem of people's cows getting in our garden. Blackie eliminated that problem ASAP.

He would follow me anywhere I went. One day, I rode my bike down to the company store and parked the bike behind the store. I went through the back entrance and left out the front of the store, caught a ride, and went home. The next day, I went to the store to get my bike. Blackie was laying there waiting for me to return.

A year or two before this, my Uncle Harry gave me a 16-gauge Iver Johnson single-shot shotgun. I killed many, many rabbits with it.

Blackie had been with us for three or four years. He was part of the family now. Maw made sure he got fed every day—sometimes not a lot, but enough.

One morning, I was going to go down the road. For what, I don't remember.

It was a little strange Blackie wasn't on the porch. I didn't think anything of it. I went through the front yard, opened the gate, and went down two or three steps, over to the left on the side of the hill. Blackie was laying there. He looked like he was asleep.

He was stiff as a board. Anytime he was coming home, he would walk about a foot from the ditch. He was smart enough to stay out of the road. The road was about 60 feet wide at this spot.

Blackie was laid to rest in a nice spot under a large tree. After the tears stopped flowing and I got myself back together, I went out in the road. I could see where someone had run out of the road at a high rate of speed and hit the dog. I looked at the tracks over and over. There was a pretty good imprint in the dirt.

I knew exactly whose car made the tracks. There was no doubt in my mind. My blood pressure was off the chart.

In the corner of the bedroom was the Iver Johnson. I put the shell in it. One was all I would need. Down the road I went. It was about a mile or mile and a half. I went up and beat on the front door, and his mother came to the door. I asked her if her son was home. She said, "No, he went to Grundy."

Since then, I have thanked the Lord many times for sending him to Grundy that day.

I hate to write this, but if he had been home, it would have been his last day on earth. I had every intention of shooting him in the center of his chest, hoping it would go deep enough to hit his heart.

He doesn't know how blessed he was that day. I was blessed also. I probably would still be in prison.

Squirrel Hunting

In the fall when hunting season opened up, we did a lot of squirrel and rabbit hunting. We never hunted when the season was closed. Not only was hunting a good sport, but also it put a lot of meat on the table. There weren't any bears, deer, or turkeys in Buchanan County at that time. When you were in the mountains, very seldom did you see a deer track. If you did, it was a rare occasion.

There are two ways to squirrel hunt. The first way is with a dog. You take the dog in the woods and turn him loose. He will do all the work. After a while, you will hear him start barking. If you follow the sound of him barking, you will find the dog sitting at the base of the tree. 99% of the time, the squirrel is up in that tree somewhere. After you see the squirrel, then *bang!* It falls out of the tree. Make sure it is dead before you pick it up.

Let the dog lick some of the blood. He will get excited and try twice as hard to tree the next one.

The second way is called still hunting. This is the only way I ever hunted squirrel. I never owned a good squirrel dog.

The best way to still hunt is early in the morning at the crack of day light. The ground is still covered in dew, so when you take a step, it doesn't make any noise. The leaves on the ground are like a cushion.

If you pick your steps very carefully, you can slip through the woods and not make one sound.

As you slip through the woods, keep your ears open. If you are lucky, soon you will hear a squirrel eating. Usually, the squirrel will be in a nut tree, hickory, walnut or beech tree. When they eat, they cut into the nut with their front teeth. The wood shavings fall to the ground. This is the sound you have been waiting to hear. Once you hear this sound, you won't forget it. It is called cutting. When a squirrel is cutting, it is a lot easier to slip upon.

Once you have slipped upon the squirrel and are under the tree, it's time to pull the trigger. You make sure the squirrel is dead. A squirrel can cut into a black walnut without any trouble. Just think what it could do to your hand.

One of the best hillbilly breakfasts that you can get is squirrel, squirrel gravy, and homemade biscuits. If you ever get the chance, don't pass it up.

My Uncle Tom was a good hunter. When he went hunting, it was a rare occasion for him to come home with nothing. Every chance he got, he was in the mountains. Early one morning, he was hunting in a large stand of hickory trees. He said there were squirrels everywhere. One tree had a hole in it about the size of a baseball. The squirrels were playing. They would run up to the hole for a few seconds and run away.

He said he kept watching, and five ran up to the hole and hesitated for a few seconds. *Bang!* He picked up four off the ground. He couldn't find the fifth one. Four out of five isn't bad. One shot kills four. Not too shabby. We had squirrel for breakfast the next couple of mornings.

One morning I was squirrel hunting up in big branch. I was slipping along as quiet as possible. After about half an hour, I heard the distinct noise of a squirrel cutting. *Slip, slip, slip, slip.* Then, I was at the tree where they were cutting. I can see two. *Bang!* One falls out and the other one runs around the tree trunk. As I moved around the tree, the squirrel moved around. I move, and the squirrel moves. Cat and mouse game. I got tired of moving and looking up. I decided to lay down and wait the squirrel out. Once he took off, I had a good chance of shooting it. I laid there for maybe 15 minutes. All of a sudden, *pop!* I got stung by a yellow jacket.

They were all over my arm. I am glad I had a jacket on. I had laid down on a yellow jacket's nest. No one had to tell me to get the hell outta there. I left my gun and the one squirrel laying there. Down the holler I went. After a while, I went back and got the gun and squirrel. I only got stung twice on the hand. The next day, my hand and arm were three times as big as they normally are. I am allergic to bee stings.

Once I was squirrel hunting, quite a way back in the woods. I was sitting on a stump about 50 feet from where there was a little bit of water running down the mountain. After a while, I heard *slip, slip, and slip.* A couple of minutes went by. Here comes a friend of mine slipping up the little creek. I sat real still, and he went on up the holler. I was afraid to say anything. He might have gotten spooked and shot me. The next time I saw him, I told him about it, and he didn't believe me for a long time.

Fishing Trip

When you are in Patterson, if you go up the road, the asphalt turns into dirt. If you keep going, the road gets real narrow. Keep going and the road goes all the way to the top of the mountain then breaks over the top and goes down the other side for about two miles. The road ends at the Slate Creek Post Office. There is a nice two-lane asphalt road there. If you turn left, that will take you to Grundy. If you turn right, that will take you to the top of Bradshaw Mountain and on into West Virginia.

Running parallel to the road is a good-sized creek. It is called Slate Creek, naturally. Once a year, Buchanan County and state of Virginia stocks the creek with trout. Then, they wait a couple of weeks or more. Then, they open fishing season. All of us boys in Patterson know when they stock the creek, and we know when the season opens. We start getting ready two or three weeks in advance.

When the big day came, we were more than ready. We got up way before daylight, got all our crap in one sack, and headed for Slate Creek walking. We left Patterson in plenty of time to get there when the season opened. You couldn't put your hook in the water before 10:00 a.m.

When we left Patterson, we were carrying fishing pole, worms, flies, knife, peanut butter sandwiches, pop, and anything else we could think of that we might need and carry.

We would fish all day. If we were lucky, we might catch one or two small ones. I don't think any of us ever caught anything big enough to keep. Late that evening we would start the long walk back home across the mountain. By the time we got home, it was way after dark. We had no fish and were starved to death, it was very late, and I still had all my chores to do. The next day, we would all talk about the fishing trip. Usually, we would decide that it wasn't worth it and that the boys on Slate Creek had already caught the big ones.

We all voted not to go back next year. But, when next year came, we all got excited and did it again.

Camping

Every now and then on the weekend, a bunch of us boys would go back into the mountains camping. We would gather up everything we would need, including blankets, water, and matches. We always took potatoes and maybe a little butter and salt. If we didn't have anything else, we could have baked potatoes and anything else we could scrape up to eat.

One of our favorite places to camp was at the old, abandoned strip mine. After the coal was harvested, it left a big, flat place. It is just right for camping, and there's no possible chance of catching anything on fire. It was also super easy to clean up our mess when we left.

This one particular time, three or four of us wanted to go, but we didn't have any food to take. Everybody knew you can't go camping without food. We were at one of the boy's houses sitting on the porch trying to come up with some bright idea. Anything is better than nothing. It just so happened that out in the yard were some chickens. One of us decided we could have chicken tonight. All we had to do was catch one. Kirby Ward lived in the next house up the holler, and the chickens belonged to him. *He won't miss one*, we thought. We all went out in the yard and cut one of the hens out of the flock and ran it under the house. We ran the hen up in a corner, and it was lights out for her. We put the old girl in a brown paper bag. No one saw us, problem solved. We all went camping as planned and had roasted chicken. The old hen was pretty tough, but it didn't stop us. Everything went very well on the trip, or so we thought. About a week later, we were all down at the company store sitting on the steps and passing around one R.C. Cola. We were BSing, tee-heeing and ha-haaing. Rut row! Here comes Kirby Ward. You could tell by the way he was walking that he was on a mission. He was coming straight for us. We all knew what he had on his mind, and it wasn't the weather. The tee-heeing and ha-haaing came to a screeching halt. He asked us how we were doing. We told him fine. After a little more small talk, he got down to the meat of the conversation—chicken. He proceeded to tell us the hen we took was one of his best layers. He could count on her laying one egg per day every day. He told us we should be ashamed of ourselves, and we should be sorry. We all told him we were sorry and apologized to him.

Then, he said if we promised him we wouldn't do a trick like that again, he wouldn't tell our parents to keep us out of trouble. We couldn't promise him fast enough and thanked him for not telling on us.

Kirby was a preacher as well as a coal miner. I think the preacher part helped us that day.

Swimming

In the summertime, a lot of days after all the chores were done, many of us boys would go swimming. There were two different places we went to. Each one was about three miles from Patterson. One was up toward Crystal Block. The water there was about four feet deep. The swimming hole was about 40 feet wide and maybe 80 feet long. There was a huge flat rock on the edge of the water. We used it as a jumping off place. If it hadn't rained in a few days, the water was so clean. If there was a dime on the bottom, you could tell whether it was heads or tails. If any of the girls from Patterson went swimming, they always went to this swimming hole. They didn't go very often.

The second place we went was straight down the road about three miles, maybe a little more. Across the road and up on the hill was a little white church. We wouldn't go swimming at the swimming hole while they were having services.

The water was seven or eight feet deep in the middle, maybe 60 feet wide and about 125 feet long. The road was about 30 or 40 feet above the water. There was also a large tree that kind of leaned out over the water. It was maybe 70 feet above the water. We would climb the tree and jump into the water.

Most of the time, we went swimming here instead of Crystal Block.

If we heard some girls might be going swimming, then we would go to Crystal Block.

About halfway between the swimming hole and home was a huge mulberry tree that hung out over the road. Every year that tree was loaded with berries. The branches were huge when the berries got ripe and started to fall. The entire road under the tree was almost black from cars running over the berries.

After we had been swimming all day, we were headed home. We were starved to death. When we got within sight of the mulberry tree, there would be a foot race to get there first.

Whoever got there first would get the most berries. When we left there, our tongues, lips, and fingers were blue. About a fourth of a mile on up the road toward home was a spring with excellent water coming straight out of the side of the mountain. Someone had made a little dam and put a piece of pipe in it. We always drank our fill after the mulberries.

When there was a drought, a lot of the people in the holler hauled water from that spring. When the water was running slow, someone would put a large galvanized clean garbage can under the pipe. When you went to get water, you didn't have to wait; you'd just dip out the water you needed. The can would gradually fill back up and be ready for the next person.

One day, I was headed swimming. All my friends were already gone. I was by myself. About a mile down the road from my house was two or three company houses. You had to cross a real narrow foot bridge to get across the creek.

The lady that lived in one of the houses hollered at me to come over there when I got there. She motioned for me to go around the back of the house. On the porch was about a 10-gallon crock full of home brew. She gave me a glass and she had one also. I think she had already had a couple. I drank the glass and was going to leave. Then, she told me to sit down and have another one. The third glass went down like water. She had changed the subject and was talking about other things. Her husband was twice as big as I was. I decided it was time for me to leave, and I did. The foot bridge to get to her house had shrunk to about half its width. When I made it across, instead of turning left to go swimming, I turned right to go home. About halfway home, I climbed up on the side of the hill under a shade tree and proceeded to get sick again and again. That was my first fight with alcohol, but definitely not my last.

Drown

There is a wide place in the road between Iaegar and Bradshaw, West Virginia. It is called Bear Town, West Virginia. Maybe there were 20 houses at the most.

My grandmaw had a brother who lived in Bear Town. His name was Burl Stanley. He had several kids and quite a few grandkids. Maw went over to visit him one weekend. It might have been the 4th of July.

Burl lived near the river. I think it was the Tug River. The local swimming hole was directly behind his house. All the kids in the neighborhood were there swimming.

The swimming hole was maybe 60 feet across by 150 feet long and maybe 8 feet deep in the middle. Everybody was having fun. This one kid wanted to go over to the other side, but he couldn't swim. I was a pretty good swimmer. So, I told him to get on my back, and I would take him across.

Everything was going well until he started to climb up on my shoulders. That pushed me under. When I went under, he climbed up high on my shoulders. By now, my head was two feet underwater. Luckily, my feet hit the bottom. When they hit the bottom, I turned around and walked back toward the bank. Pretty soon, I came to where the water wasn't over my head. That was the last time I tried that trick.

The good Lord was watching over me and my passenger. Thank you, Lord.

Shower and Outhouse

In our backyard close to the house was a root cellar. It was almost completely buried in the side of mountain. The front was sticking out, the back was covered, and most of the two sides were covered with dirt. If you kept the door shut, it stayed cool inside even during the summer. We stored potatoes, apples, and onions in it. When Maw canned anything, it went inside the cellar. It was about 10 feet by 10 feet with a cement floor and cinder block sides.

On top of the cellar was a smoke house. We used it as a catch-all for all of our junk. Anything I thought I might have needed, I brought it home.

This is where I took a shower once a week, whether I needed it or not, usually on Saturday. The shower head was a five-gallon can with five or six holes punched in the bottom. You fill the can with water and hang it up really quick, and you have a shower. The holes in the can were very small so it lasted quite a while. I could take a complete shower with one can full. You had to really hurry. I was also standing in a Number 3 washtub to catch the water. In the wintertime, we put the tub behind the heating stove. That was the warmest place in the whole house. In the winter, I tried to take a shower at the miner's bath house.

We had five rooms and a path. The path went to the outhouse. It was maybe 125 feet from the house. Our main supplies of toilet paper were the Sears and Roebuck Company and the Montgomery Ward Company catalogs. When we got a new catalog in the mail, if you wanted to look at it, you'd better hurry. It was headed for the outhouse. It didn't take long for you to figure out to use the brown and white or the black and white pages first. They were soft compared to the colored pages. The colored pages were hard on the old boongie, and they did not clean as good.

In the wintertime when it was freezing outside and you had to go, you knew you could only put it off for so long. When you were in the outhouse, you didn't sit out there and daydream. Have you ever heard the old saying, "Shit and get?" Now, you know where that comes from.

Sometime in the summer, I would see my sister going to the outhouse. Imagine if you sat in the outhouse doing your business and daydreaming, and you were totally unaware of anything. I would get a rock about half the size of a baseball and throw it very hard and hit the side of the crapper. She would be sitting in there and suddenly, *bam!* If she was dozing, she was definitely awake now. I know if she would have caught me, she would have choked the crap out of me.

My grandmaw had two big bookends. Well, my sister and I got into a little scuffle over a dime. She had hidden it under one of these bookends. When I discovered where she hid it, there was a mad dash for the dime. During the scuffle, one of the bookends fell on my big toe. I didn't have any shoes on. It really hurt, and I forgot about the dime. I think it was payback for me hitting the outhouse with rocks. My big toenail was black for a long time.

Attending Church

In the '50s, up in the holler, there were two churches. One was the Church of Christ. This church had a cemetery up on the hill behind the church. Some of the graves had little houses built over them. Other than one church having a cemetery and one not, don't ask me what the difference was. I do not know. I was never in the Church of Christ. When they had dinner on the ground, though, I was always there.

They were both small churches, maybe 75 people on a real good Sunday. When I did go, which wasn't very often, I went to the Church of God.

Once a week, they would have service at night. I think it was called Bible Study. It was geared toward the younger generation—pre-teens and teenagers. One of the things we did was called scripture scramble. We would all split up into two groups, maybe called the "red team" and the "blue team." Each team's group would sit on one side or the other side of the aisle.

Everyone would have a Bible. Someone up front would call out a scripture, such as John 3:16. As soon as the MC called out John, everyone would start looking for it. The first person in either group to find it would jump up and read it out loud. That group would get one point. They would keep score for maybe eight or ten weeks, and the team that had the most points would win a small prize.

Another game we played was when the MC would have maybe 20 or 30 questions, such as, "How many books are in the New Testament?" If a person jumped up with the right answer, then they scored one point for their team. If the person got it wrong, one point was deducted from their team. This was something to do one night a week. All of us boys knew when church was over. All the girls would need someone to walk them home. We asked the girls way before church was over so there wouldn't be any disappointment, or some other boy wouldn't get ahead of you.

When we walked them home, we walked really slow to make it last longer. If we were lucky, then we would get a good night kiss. If the mother or dad was waiting on the porch, your luck just ran out.

At some of the evening services for adults and after the lengthy preaching, some of the congregation would go up front. They would start singing. After a few songs, they would raise their hands toward Heaven and start rocking back and forth and singing all the while. Most of them would have their eyes closed. Then, they would start speaking in unknown tongues, whirling around and dancing, swaying back and forth, some would be shouting, and some would be still singing. Some would sink down and be laying in the floor. The ones in the floor would be speaking in unknown tongues, bouncing up and down, squirming and jerking. I was surprised they didn't hurt themselves. This went on for about 15 or 20 minutes.

After a while, they would settle down and, one by one, they would get up and go back to their seats. After everyone was seated, the preacher would say a few more words. Then, they sang a hymn or two, and the service was over.

Snake Handling Church

If you were in Patterson and you wanted to go to the snake handling church, then you had to go to Jolo, West Virginia. You would go all the way up to the head of the holler, cross the top of the mountain and down the other side to the Slate Creek Post Office. Then, you would turn right and go all the way up to the top of Bradshaw Mountain. On top of the mountain is the Virginia and West Virginia state line. My friend and I bought many, many gallons of moonshine liquor up there. But that is for another chapter. You go down the other side of Bradshaw Mountain, and then you are in West Virginia. When you get to the bottom of the mountain, go a few miles more, and you'll come to a little community called Jolo.

Before I move forward, I want to be clear that this is not being written to make fun of or degrade these people. They have their own way of worship. I have been to the church many, many times and would again if I got the chance.

The people that attend this church believe in handling snakes—not pet snakes, and not garden or black snakes. I am talking real live rattlesnakes and copperheads. These snakes were caught in the mountains, and they have never made a trip to a snake dentist either. Big snakes with big teeth and fangs! These snakes aren't babies. They are very big. Like I said, I have been many times to the church. The answer to your question is, "No, I have never handled a snake at the church." Every time I went, I sat in the back, as in the *last* row.

From the outside, it looks just like any other Southern church. When they are handling the snakes, they believe that if you get bit, and you have enough faith in the Lord, the snake bite won't hurt you.

The service starts, and the preacher preaches for a while. The service is very similar to the Church of God in Patterson, so far. After the preacher has been preaching for a while, six or eight of the congregation will go up front and start singing and playing music. They have a guitar, banjo, tambourine, piano, and maybe another instrument or two. The music has a very strong beat. Let me tell you, the music is as good as any music I have ever heard. It is as good or better than any concert that I have ever been to.

There was a homemade wooden box about 18 inches by 18 inches, maybe 8 inches deep with a lid on top with hinges. While the music was playing and there was singing going on, one of the people up front opened the lid. The person then reached into the box and brought out a good-sized snake, maybe a timber rattler, sometimes referred to as a diamond back rattler.

The person that has the snake will hand it to someone else, then reach into the box and get another one out, and hand it to someone else. He kept pulling them out of the box, and there were six or eight being passed around. While they were holding the snakes, they were still singing and dancing around. The music never stops. Sometimes, one person may have had three or four snakes at one time. The people who handled the snakes were definitely not afraid.

While all of this was going on, someone brought out a quart fruit jar. Inside the jar was a white liquid and it looked like watered-down milk.

They took the lid off the jar and poured the lid full of the liquid. They passed it around. One person would take a sip and make a really bad face. Then, they passed it on to the next person. They would take a sip, make a bad face, and pass it on. What do you think they were drinking? The answer is at the end of this chapter.

One time I was there, and there were about eight or ten college students. I think they were from Cherry Hill, North Carolina, Bible College. They had their pads and pencils out, maybe a camera or two. There were no smart phones back then. You would be lucky if you found a phone within a 10-mile radius.

The pastor of the church was a lady. After she had preached for a while, the kids continued to take notes. She stopped the sermon and told them in no uncertain terms, "This is not a circus, and this is not a sideshow. If you want to participate, then come on up here to the front. If you don't want to participate, sit down." I have never seen a bunch of young people sit down so fast in my life. They got an education that night.

On another occasion, I was with my Uncle Dick, and we decided to go over to Jolo to the snake handling church. When we got over there, Dick decided he wasn't going to go in. I told him I came all the way over here to go to the church, and I am going to go in. He decided he would go inside with me. Then, we went in and sat down in the back of the church. I think he held his feet up off the floor the entire time we were in there.

After Uncle Dick and I left there, on the way home, we stopped at a beer joint. I had never been there before in my life. You could hear the band playing when we stopped in the parking lot. When we got up to the door, the bouncer stopped us. They told Uncle Dick they would let him in if he promised not to dance with any of the chairs. Also, when the music was playing, he couldn't holler. Uncle Dick promised he would be good, so they let us in.

I am not into snakes, but I did enjoy going to their church. These people have more faith in the Lord than 99% of anyone else I know. The white liquid they were drinking was strychnine!

Going to the Hospital

As far back as I can remember, I knew I had a heart problem. Sometimes, while lying in the bed, my heartbeat would shake the whole bed. I had lived with this my whole life, so it didn't bother me too much. I definitely didn't worry about it. I learned what worrying would do for you. I had watched my mother get sick and have a nervous breakdown.

I learned how to concentrate and slow my heartrate down. My heart would beat three or four times or maybe a dozen regular beats, then it would stop for two or three seconds. Then, it would beat one hard time. I could feel this beat at the ends of my fingers and toes. I could feel this coming on two or three minutes before it happened.

If this got really bad and I couldn't make it slow down, then I would hit the aspirin bottle pretty hard. Usually, that would help.

One night, it got really bad. The aspirin wouldn't phase it. Nothing I did would bring it back to the normal beat. If I didn't get some help, I wouldn't see the sunrise. I thought I was going to have the big one. I got out of bed and walked to my friend Junior's house. I woke him up. I told him I needed to go to the hospital right now.

Junior woke his dad and told him my problem. He gave Junior the car keys, and off we went to the hospital in Grundy. When we got to the hospital, we went into the emergency room. I told the nurse my problem and that I needed a doctor ASAP.

She sent me down into the basement. I started looking for the room she had told me to go to. As I went down the hall, there was a man lying on a gurney. He looked like a coal miner. He was looking straight at me. I said hello or hi or something. I didn't hear him answer me.

I find the room and the doctor. He had me sit up on a table that had no padding at all. He listened to my heart here and there in the front part of my body. Then, he listened and did the same thing on my back. While he listened to my heart, he asked a few questions.

It didn't take him two minutes to diagnose me. The doctor told me to quit drinking, sober up, and I would be okay. I told him I hadn't had anything to drink, and I didn't drink at all. He told me to button up my shirt and go home. He left me sitting on the table, walked out of the room, and he was gone. After I got myself together, I went back down the hall, and that guy was still lying on the gurney. When I passed him, he looked at me straight in the eye again. I spoke to him again, but he didn't answer.

Junior and I went back to Patterson, and he dropped me off at home. I think that was the longest night of my life. I was sure glad to see the break of day. More on this later. You can't make this up.

Looking back on that night, I think the nurse sent me downstairs to the morgue, and the doctor I saw was the County Coroner. The coal miner lying on the gurney, I think, was dead. That was the first dead person I had ever seen with their eyes open.

Christmas Cards & Cleo

About two months before Christmas, maybe October or early November, I would go around to all the houses in the holler taking orders for boxes of Christmas cards.

I usually did pretty good. I think it was mostly because they felt sorry for me.

After everyone settled with me, I made a few dollars. That was a little gold mine for me. A few dollars are a lot better than no dollars.

I had an Aunt Cleo, and she worked at the Sears and Roebuck in Norfolk, VA. All year long, she would gather up anything and everything. Any time something came through Sears—returns, scratch and dent, anything that was a bargain that she thought we could use—she couldn't pass it up.

She and her husband, Herman, always spent Christmas with us. When they arrived at our house, you would think Santa just landed. The car was completely packed. The trunk was full, and the back seat was so full that Herman could not see out of the rear-view mirror.

Maw and Cleo would pass out all the stuff to all the family members. No one was left out.

Maw would pick out some things and hold them back after the dust and excitement settled down. The next day, she would take the things she kept back and go around to the neighbors, especially the neediest, and make sure they got a little something.

Grit

Up on the hill, behind the company store, were about four or five houses. This is where the mine superintendent and bosses lived. The last house in the row lived Burl and Hassie Matney. I don't know what position Burl had, but I do know that he worked at the mine.

His wife, Hassie, was in a league all by herself. I think in her first life, she was a sailor. To say she had a foul mouth wouldn't come close to describing her language. If she was in a cussing contest, she would win a prize every time. She was a big woman, maybe 300 pounds, and she didn't take any lip from anyone, which included her old man, Burl. When she got wound up, he couldn't get a word in edgewise. I felt a little sorry for him.

I had a friend who was trying to sell magazine subscriptions to make himself a little money. He would go door-to-door and pitch the magazines. One of the magazines' names was "Grit." It was very popular back then.

Joe goes up on the hill and beats on Burl and Hassie's door. Hassie opened the door and asked him, "What the hell do you want?" Joe said, "I am selling Grit." Before he can get the word "magazine" out, or any of the rest of his pitch, Hassie started and said, "You are selling shit. What in the G-d— h— would make you think I want to buy some shit?" She went on and on, ranting and raving. When she finished, she started smiling, hesitated for a few seconds, and told him she would like to buy a one-year subscription.

Joe was almost in tears but smiling because she gave him an order for three different magazines.

Maytag

My Grandmaw had a Maytag washing machine with the wringer on top. Inside the machine was an agitator. You put the dirty clothes in the top with some soap and shut the lid. On the side was a red knob. Pull the red knob out, and the washing machine started. When you think the clothes were clean, you push the red knob in, and the machine stops. No automatic on and off here. Next, you open the lid and, piece by piece, you run the clothes through the wringer. Do not get your fingers caught in the wringer. If you do, it hurts like hell. I guarantee you won't let it happen again. When the clothes go through the wringer, they fall into a large tub of clean water. Stir them around a little bit, and then run them through the wringer again. Put them in the clothes basket, and they are now ready to be hung up on the clothesline.

Maw's clothesline was stretched from a post on the front porch to the pine tree in the yard, maybe 50 or 60 feet. When she hung the clothes on the line and it was sagging, she always had a clothes pole to use. It was about eight feet long with a fork on the end or a nail driven about half-way in. You put the clothesline in the fork on the clothes pole and prop it up.

At this time, Maw was doing wash for four or five people. My Uncle Dick, Uncle Harry, and Aunt Jackie were still living at home. My Uncle Tom was married and had his own family.

Groundhog

During hunting season, Dick and Harry were in the mountains every chance they got. They were always bringing home squirrels and rabbits. A lot of the time, I got the job of skinning and cleaning them. After a while, I got good, then fast.

One day, one of them brought home a baby groundhog. It was so small. Maw had to feed it with an eye dropper. With all the care it was getting, it was growing like a weed. When it was about ⅓ grown, it would sit up on its hind legs and eat a popsicle or fudgesicle, holding the stick with its front paws.

It was so tame that if you sat down for a few minutes, it would crawl up in your lap and you could pet it like a cat. Every Monday morning, Maw started washing clothes. You wouldn't get in her way, because she was on a mission to get the clothes washed and hung out. The clothes were already sorted out. The washing machine had hot water and Tide in it. She went and got a huge armful of white clothes and put them in the washer. She shut the lid and pulled out the red knob. After 15 or 20 minutes, Maw decided the clothes were washed enough and were clean. She pushed the red knob in, and the washer quit. She raised the lid, and the first thing she saw was the baby groundhog floating around on top of the clothes.

Everyone really felt bad, especially Maw. She wrapped it up in a large piece of cloth. I took it a little way up the mountain and buried it.

No more baby groundhogs in Maw's house after that.

Bus

When we passed the seventh grade, we went to Grundy High School. We rode the school bus 16 miles to school and 16 miles home. The bus was a well-used 1948 Ford. It looked like it had been through the war with a lot of battle scars. We called it "Old Number 2."

The trip to Grundy wasn't a piece of cake. The road was very crooked and went up and down the little hills. After a while, that 16 miles got longer and longer.

We had some good times on the old bus. Occasionally, someone would swipe a roll of toilet paper from the bathroom at school and bring it on the bus. We waited until after we got out of town a couple of miles, because we knew not to do anything in town. Next, some kid would put the window in the back down and let the toilet paper unroll out the window.

Shut your eyes and just imagine seeing an old rickety school bus full of kids going down the road with a string of toilet paper 30 or 40 feet long hanging out the back window, flapping in the breeze.

For years and years, our bus driver was Mr. Sloan. He had to be made from good material to stand up to being the bus driver on the Patterson route. Besides us unruly kids, the old bus had no power steering, no air conditioning, very little heat, and was a standard shift. When we went up a little hill, he would have to down shift just to make it to the top.

About six or eight of us boys caught the bus at the four-room school.

One morning, a wild duck flew into one of the school windows and killed itself. One of my amigos put the duck in a brown paper bag and took it on the school bus. All of us boys sat in the back of the bus most of the time. After a while, maybe halfway to Grundy, someone threw the duck toward the front and hollered, "Duck!"

I don't know how, but it missed all the kids and hit Mr. Sloan in the back of the head. He slowed the bus down, pulled over, and stopped. Mr. Sloan stood up, got the brown paper bag, and held it up for all of us to see. He asked, "Is this someone's lunch?" No one answered. So, he looked in the bag and said, "Oh, pishaw!" He opened the door, tossed it out, shut the door, sat back down, and continued to Grundy.

The old bus broke down a few times, but overall, it was very dependable. Old Number 2 was the oldest bus in the whole fleet. It got me there and back for about four years.

I'm sure that between all of us kids and the rag bus, it took its toll on Mr. Sloan. I don't know what pay was like for bus drivers back then, but whatever Mr. Sloan made, it wasn't enough.

Cash Register

There was a mom-and-pop store in Patterson for a few years. I think it was run by Ras Kinder and his wife, but mostly his wife. It was your typical one-horse store. They had all the staples, which included milk, bread, and lunch meats. They did not have vegetables. A large amount of junk food such as candy, cakes, pies, chips, ice cream, and pop were also available. In addition, a large assortment of cigarettes and chewing tobacco could be found. All the important stuff could be purchased.

They had a pinball machine that was very important to us. Any time one of us boys got a nickel—not a spare nickel, because there were no spare nickels anywhere in the holler—it went into the pinball machine. It did not take us long to figure out how to beat the machine. We would put a nickel in and hit the machine in a certain spot and, *ding, ding, ding!* It would give you three or four free games. If we were careful, we could play for hours on one nickel.

One hot summer day, about three or four of us boys were sitting outside of the store in the shade enjoying a R.C. Cola and BSing.

Suddenly, we heard this super loud crash that came from inside the store. Then, we heard a kid scream at the top of his lungs. The lady that ran the store had her three-year-old boy in the store with her. We all ran in the store to see what happened. There were pennies, nickels, dimes, and quarters everywhere, and the cash register was laying in the floor. She had her son in her arms with blood all over the side of his head, and it was still flowing.

There weren't any rags or towels to stop the bleeding. I give the lady credit because she did something no man would've thought of. She grabbed a box of Kotex pads and immediately placed one of them on the child's head. That stopped the bleeding immediately. Within 15 minutes, the store was locked, and she and the little boy were on their way to the Grundy Hospital. I'll give her credit, she didn't panic. She took control of the situation and handled it perfectly.

The lady always left the drawer to the cash register open so she wouldn't have to ring up every nickel that she took in. The little boy was trying to climb up onto the counter. He got ahold of the cash drawer and pulled the cash register off the counter. If it had fallen directly on top of him, it would have been much worse. The cash register was big enough to handle the Neiman Marcus Store in New York City.

When the cash register hit the little boy, it cut about a three-inch gash almost on the top of his head. When I first saw the cut and the way it was bleeding, it scared the crap out of me. The boy lost a lot of blood in a very short time.

When they got back from the hospital, he looked like the "Sheik of Arabia." He had enough gauze and tape wrapped around his head to outfit a young army.

Cleaning Poop and Doctoring Animals

Maw was always good with animals. If something was on its death bed, she would doctor it up. Pretty soon, it would come back to life. I can't remember a time when she didn't have a cat. We never had a mouse problem. Occasionally, her cat would get sick and throw up. One way to tell if a cat is sick is that it will eat grass. After a short while, the cat will throw the grass back up. Maw had a little box of white powder. No, it was not cocaine. She called it "coppers." She would take a sharp pointed knife and stick the point of blade into the powder and get a teeny tiny bit on the knife and mix it in warm milk. Then, she would feed it to the cat. The next day, the cat would be just fine.

I don't know what was in the coppers, where it came from, or the manufacturer. But I do know whatever it was, it worked.

Sometimes when Maw wasn't looking, I would catch the cat sleeping on the linoleum floor. I would get a piece of tape about three or four inches long and put it across the cat's tail. Then, I would stick the two ends to the floor. It's about time for the action to start. "Here, Kitty, Kitty." The cat thought it was going to get some table scraps. It would jump up and try to take off. The cat looked like it was in four-wheel drive. Its paws were spinning 90 miles per hour, but it wasn't going anywhere. Maw would have had a fit if she had caught me.

A few other times, I would be petting the cat while it was stretched out on the floor. I would put my finger under the cat's chin and spin it around and around about six or eight times. When I quit, the cat would walk away. You would swear it was drunk.

Neither one of these little tricks hurt the cat. Believe me, if I had hurt Maw's cat, there would be hell to pay. She couldn't stand and wouldn't stand for any kind of animal to be hurt.

Like I said, Maw could doctor up anything. She would have made a great vet. When little chicks first hatch out, they are covered in yellow down (fuzz). They follow the mother hen everywhere. They scratch and pick all day long, always looking for something to eat. Sometimes when the chicks are really small and when they poop a little bit, it doesn't make it all the way off the chick. Then it dries on the chick. The next time the little chick poops, a little bit more stays on the chick and dries. After a few days, the poop has built up and shuts the door. Therefore, the chicks can't poop at all. This is a death sentence unless something is done and done quick. Here comes Maw to the rescue. She would catch one at a time and perform boongie surgery. She would hold the chick upside down in her left hand. With her right hand, she would take a pair of scissors and trim all the poop off and all the fuzz around the chick's boongie. Then, she would take soapy water and wash it real gently. Next, she would pat it dry with a towel, put a little Vaseline on it, and turn it loose. Then, she would catch another one and do it all over again. After the operation, the chick was good for its entire childhood.

One day at school during lunch, one of the kids spotted a chicken across the creek near the railroad. They started throwing rocks at it. The chicken ran into some bushes for protection. The chicken got hung up in the bushes and couldn't run. After the kids threw a ton of rock, the bell rang to end lunch hour. Lucky for the chicken. When school was out, everyone forgot about the white chicken, except me. After we all went home, I went back to school, jumped the creek, and retrieved the chicken. It was in very bad shape. It had lost one eye and couldn't stand up. A cat has nine lives. Some chickens have more than one.

Maw went to work on it. A little here and a little there. After about a week, it was getting around pretty good and mingling with the rest of the flock. After maybe a month, we started getting one large white egg per day. Every day just like clockwork, we got an egg. We got dozens of eggs from that hen. She paid Maw back many times over.

One of Maw's other hens had made a nest in an old rotted-out tree stump. She was sitting on 12 eggs. One day, I went out to get a bucket of coal and saw the hen up on top of the stump flapping her wings, squawking and making a big commotion. Something must be wrong! Usually, the hen is down in the stump sitting on the eggs. I go up there and looked down in the stump. There was a big black snake curled up on top of the eggs, swallowing them whole, one at a time. I went back to the house as fast as I could run. I told Maw what the problem was, and she dropped everything. She went to the nightstand drawer and got her trusty .38. She loaded it with six bullets and headed for the stump. The hen was still having a fit. When Maw got there and saw the snake, *bang!* No more black snake problem. I got the snake out of the stump and stretched it out in the road. It was almost four foot long. You could see two large bulges in the snake. It had already eaten two eggs and was working on the third. Like they say in sniper school, "One shot, one kill." About two or three weeks later, we had nine little chicks. In about three or four months, those nine chicks equaled nine Sunday fried chicken dinners. Southern fried chicken dinners are the best.

Fan

The main road that went up through Patterson went all the way to the top of the mountain and down to Slate Creek, where it ended. About a mile up the road from the company store, a smaller road turned off and went up into Horn Hollow. I lived in one corner of that intersection. When someone asked me where in Patterson I lived, I told them I lived at the mouth of Horn Holler.

About half a mile up in Horn Holler, there was one house and one cinder block building. There was a large steel door with a huge padlock. Around the side of the mountain about one hundred feet, the mines had opened a drift mouth in the seam of coal. This was used as an airway to the inside of the mine.

There was a huge fan, maybe six foot in diameter, mounted on a concrete pad. It had two cinder block sides and a concrete roof. It was built into the side of the hill so it would only suck dirty air out of the mines. Clean air was coming into the mine from another open drift mouth maybe two miles away. Any smoke or gas that was generated inside the mine was replaced with clean air quick.

Early in the morning before the fog lifted, everything was quiet from my house, I could hear the fan running. This was a way for me to know if the mines were working that day. Some days when I was up there, if it was hot out, I would stand in front of the fan and get cooled off. The temperature inside the mines was a constant temperature of summer and winter.

The little cinder block building was where all the controls were for the fan. The steel door and padlock were there to keep everyone out. The only house in the holler was a company house. The family that lived there had the last name of Horn. The holler was named after the old man. He was the keeper of the key to the controls. That was his job.

Mr. Horn had about four or five kids. The oldest boy was a couple of years older than me. I don't remember him ever going to school. His name was Earl.

When I was up in the holler picking up coal out of the slate dump, many times he would be picking up coal for his house. If he got his buckets full before I got the tub on my wagon full, he would help me fill the tub. I don't know for sure, but I think his daddy really mistreated Earl a lot and whipped him with a piece of cable. I would like to know if he is still living.

Buggy Ride

My grandmaw was pretty straightlaced. I never remember her ever saying a bad word. If she heard you say one, then she would tell you about it, and she did not want to hear that kind of language.

My grandpaw, Tom Trent, passed away in 1946. Maw had been a widow for many years. I never ever remember her saying anything about getting another man in her life.

One day, we were sitting at the kitchen table talking about Grandpaw and old times. That was very interesting to me. I asked her, "Did Grandpaw come courting you before you were married?" She said he rode a horse and was very handsome sitting up there. I asked her, "What did you all do when he came courting?" She told me they sat on the porch in the swing and talked. Sometimes, they would go for a buggy ride. I asked her if they went for buggy rides in the winter. Yes, they went for buggy rides in the winter.

Next, I asked her how they stayed warm. She said they took a heavy blanket and wrapped it around them.

Maw was not ready for my next question. I asked, "Did Grandpaw ever try to sneak a feel?" You would have thought I had committed a mortal sin by her reaction. She jumped up from the table and grabbed the broom. I knew I was in trouble. Any time Maw got the broom after you, she meant business! She ran me out of the house. She said I was ornery and had a nasty mind and that if she could catch me, she would wash my mouth out with soap.

Forest Fires

When coal is mined, a lot of slate gets mixed in. The coal was processed in the tipple. The slate was separated from the coal in the tipple. Then, the slate was hauled away and dumped in a big pile. Some good coal and coal dust was hauled away with the slate. It was usually hauled up in a small holler and dumped.

Every day the mines worked, more slate was generated and hauled up in the holler and dumped on the pile. After two or three years, the slate dump had thousands of tons of slate and hundreds of tons of highly combustible coal.

The sun shined on the slate dump day after day, and the rain soaked everything. The sun heated the dump, and the rain was making steam. The coal was black and soaked up more sun. After a few years in the early morning, you could see steam and heat rising. Then, a week or two later, you could see just a faint bit of smoke rising. As the days went on, the smoke was noticeable. After a few more days at night, you could see the flames. This was spontaneous combustion. The dump burned for years and years.

When the fire burned out to the edge of the dump and there were dry leaves, they caught fire. This was one of the main causes of forest fires. Sometimes, it did not take very long for the fire to really get going and cause considerable damage. At night, you could see the string of fires on the sides of the mountains.

It looked kind of pretty. It looked like the mountain had a necklace on.

We were all in school one day at the four-room school. It was just another ordinary day, just like all the rest. I think we had just finished saying the pledge of allegiance and had sat back down. It was about 8:15 or 8:20 in the morning. A green pick-up truck came screeching to a halt right in front of the steps of the school. It had a big round Virginia logo on the door. One guy got out who had a green ballcap on, with a green shirt and green pants too. He was not a coal miner—that was for sure.

He came up on the porch and into the room. He didn't knock; he just opened the door and came in. You could tell he was on a mission.

He went up to Mr. Perkins' desk, and they had a conversation. I couldn't hear what was said. I thought one of us boys had done something and were in deep doo-doo.

All boys 16 years old and older were to go with him to fight a forest fire. We were to leave our desk as it was. Someone would put our books away, and if we had a packed lunch, we were to take it with us.

We all went out and piled in the back of the truck, and away we went. The mountain had caught on fire from the slate dump.

When we got to the fire, it was burning along the ground, not up in the trees. We were given a rake and told to rake the fire down the hill two or three feet away where the fire had already burned. What we raked down would soon burn itself out. This process worked really well. The guy in the green hat had done this before. It was very hot and dusty. We were working fast. It didn't take long before this turned into real work. For lunch, they fed us a can of Vienna sausage and a bottle of pop.

That evening, I knew I did not want to be a firefighter. We must have done a good job. The next day they did not come and get us. Later, we learned that the day we worked got the fire under control. The state of Virginia got a lot of free labor that day.

Movies

If we wanted to go to the movies on the weekend, we had to start early in the week, scraping up enough money so we could be flush with cash ($2.00 each) by Saturday night. We would take a small mattock and dig may apple, red root, ginseng, and one more root that I can't remember.

We would take the roots and wash all the dirt off and put them on top of the woodshed in the sun to dry out. The ginseng brought a lot of money, but it was very hard to find.

We would gather up pop bottles. We did most of the gathering after dark. All the pop bottles sitting on people's back porches didn't get a chance to gather very much dust. They would bring two cents apiece at the company store. We would pick up copper out of the slate dump. The coal mine used a lot of small copper wire to set off dynamite. After we gathered all we could find, we built a small fire and put the wire in the fire. It didn't take long to burn the insulation off the wire. Then, you had 100% copper. The copper was one of our better moneymakers.

We did anything we could to get enough money to pay for the ticket.

None of us boys were lazy. If one of us got an odd job, all of us would help him get it done. Cash money was hard to come by. Sometimes, we would really have to scrape the bottom of the barrel.

Across from the company store was a shed where they kept the truck that hauled the slate away from the tipple to the slate dump. They filled the truck with gas on certain days. So, we knew which days it was full of gas. We only visited the truck when we were low on funds. Then, we would only borrow two or three gallons. We thought if the truck was full and we only borrowed two to three gallons, no one would miss it, hopefully.

One of the boys borrowed his dad's car. That car was our main source of transportation. One night, after we had been to the movies, we had a few dollars between us. We all decided to go up to Garden Creek. There was a little drive-in restaurant up there where a lot of girls hung out. Much more was happening in Garden Creek. Nothing was going on in Patterson.

About 10 or 12 miles from Grundy, the road forked. If you went left, you went to Patterson. If you stayed on Route 460 and went right, that took you to Garden Creek. In the mountains, you don't turn east, west, north, or south. You go the way the road goes.

As soon as you bore right, there was a long bridge. It was maybe three hundred feet long. It was the Dismal Bridge. A few years ago, before this particular night, a gas truck missed the bridge and landed on the riverbank. The truck burned for hours and hours. The driver was killed. We rode the school bus the day after, and we could see the truck. It remained down there for a long time.

On the night we were going to Garden Creek and crossed this bridge, there was someone walking toward us on the side of the road. They had a cape on with a hoodie. Their arms were crossed and up in the opposite sleeve.

All of us looked at the person, but no one saw a face. The Dismal Bridge is out in the middle of nowhere. There shouldn't be anybody walking on this bridge at this time of night. We all discussed this quickly, and we decided to turn around and go back across the bridge. When we got to the end of bridge, we turned around. It couldn't have been more than three or four minutes. We went back across the bridge. There was no one on the bridge! When we got to the other end, we turned back and crossed it one more time.

Still, no one was there. Then, we went on to Garden Creek to the drive-in and nursed a coke until there wasn't anything to nurse. When we left Garden Creek, we had to cross the bridge again. We did not see anything.

Just past the Dismal Bridge going toward Garden Creek, there was a long dip in the road. At the bottom of the dip was a beer joint called "Mabel's Place." The lady that owned it was called Mabel, of course. One night, there was a really bad accident in front of Mabel's Place, and Mabel was killed. I can't recall if the accident was before we saw someone on the bridge or after.

That place is no longer there. When they made Route 460 into a four-lane road, the long dip was filled. The road is level there now. I have crossed the Dismal Bridge hundreds of times since then and have never seen anyone on the bridge. I don't know what I saw that night. I had 20/20 vision then, and I know I saw something!

We all saw something. I don't believe in ghosts. It is still a mystery.

Pat

One of my mother's sisters was named Pat. She grew up during the Depression. Her growing up in this era was probably 99% of the reason I can write this little chapter of this book. Pat resembled my mother greatly. At a distance, it was hard to tell them apart.

She was a nurse in World War II and served in North Africa for a while. I saw her scrapbook, and there were pictures of men stacked up like cord wood. Some had no legs, some had no arms, and some had no heads. She was given a medal by the President of the United States for her service on the battlefield.

When she got out of the service, she got a job at the Logan General Hospital. She rose through the ranks and became the head nurse. After she retired there, she got a job as a nurse for Logan County Health Department. During that time, a coal slurry impoundment dam burst and washed away many people, houses, and anything in its path. It was called the Buffalo Creek Flood and was on February 26, 1972. The dam was located on a hillside in the county of Logan, West Virginia. Pat received an accommodation for her service during that disaster. She also had a bridge named in honor of her services in the community of Logan and for her services as a veteran serving in North Africa. The bridge is called the "U.S. Army ILT Patricia Simon Memorial Bridge."

When she passed away, she was 92 years old. She would never tell her age. When she passed away, I think she still had 78 cents of the first dollar she made. That was when taxes were 22%.

When she went shopping, if it wasn't on sale or buy one get one free, she did not buy anything. I think Dial soap was her favorite. If it was on sale, she would buy a couple dozen bars. Then, she would take the wrappers off, put the bars in a potato sack and hang them up to dry out for a month or two. They would get as hard as a rock. They lasted a long time. She would squeeze a buffalo nickel until it crapped.

My mother, sister, and I spent one winter with her. She lived in Logan, West Virginia, with her husband, Henry, and her only son, Stan. I remember walking to school. The chalk boards at the school were not black. They were green with yellow chalk. My teacher's name was Mrs. Fitzgibbits.

The year we stayed in Logan was one of the worst years of my life. I am sure my mother and sister felt the same way.

Aunt Pat was probably miserable also, having three extra people in her house. She probably breathed a sigh of relief when we left. Thank you, Aunt Pat, for the room and board.

Peach Brandy

The company store had a policy concerning fruits and vegetables and when they got a little old. If they thought they couldn't sell them, then they always threw them out in the trash pile. Once, they had a big bunch of peaches that were very ripe and on the verge of rotting that were thrown in the dump.

Junior and I seized this rare opportunity. We gathered them all up, almost a bushel's worth, and took them to my house. We put them in the smoke house. My grandmaw had a ten-gallon crock pot that just happened to be empty. It was sitting in the smoke house and just waiting for us. We prepared the peaches and put them in the crock pot. They looked good. I think we confiscated a 10-pound bag of sugar and added that to the mix. Next, we added quite a bit of water. Then, somewhere, we had to buy some yeast. This about broke the bank. We put a rag over it to keep away flies, gnats, or any other foreign object out of our mix.

Every few days, we would sample it. The taste was bad. We were hoping it would get better. After about six weeks, we could not wait any longer. We decided it was time. The cover we had wasn't doing its job. There were flies, gnats, honeybees, many yellow jackets, and a wide variety of bugs that had not even been named yet. We had too much invested to quit now, though. We got an empty quart fruit jar and put a rag over the top and strained out a quart. We drank as much as we could stand.

That was the worst tasting stuff I had ever tasted. I didn't get a buzz, but I did get a headache really bad. It was a miracle we did not die from food poisoning. I think we poured the rest of it out. It probably killed the grass in all directions.

Commodities

Du   uring the real hard times when the mines were almost at a stand-
      still, the government would pass out commodities. My Uncle
      Dick had a contract to haul them to different locations. At a pre-
determined place and time, everyone that wanted them would go and get in
line. The line was long, and you knew everyone in line.

I think you told them how many people were in your family, and you
received a certain amount per person.

Beans, rice, powdered milk, powdered eggs, cheese, and cans of beef
and gravy were handed out. The beef and gravy looked like army rations. It
looked very good, also. The cheese came in large blocks and was unsliced. It
was also very good. I ate a lot of cheese sandwiches.

If you made a grilled cheese and toasted it, the cheese didn't melt like
Velveeta cheese did. It stayed firm. Maw would make mashed potatoes. She
put the beef and gravy over the potatoes. It was very tasty, and I liked it. She
would mix a quart of powdered milk with a quart of real milk. It wasn't the
best that ever was, but when you are hungry, just about anything tastes good.
The powdered eggs left a lot to be desired, but the price was right.

We ate a great deal of bologna. Maw would fry it. While it was frying,
she would cut the edges about one inch toward the middle of the slice. This
kept it from crinkling up like bacon. The hillbilly's name for bologna is
"round steak."

I had a friend and, in the summer, when school was out, he got a job in a slaughterhouse. He told me he got a real eye-opening education while he worked there. Before he worked there, he loved bologna sandwiches and Vienna sausages straight out of the can. After the first summer, he couldn't eat any more of either one. He said when the slaughterhouse made bologna, they didn't waste anything. The only thing they did not put in the bologna was the cow's moo.

Home Life and Chores

ome life in Patterson was very hard. But us kids did not know any different. We were poor; we just didn't know how poor we really were. Most of the families in the holler were in the same boat. Our main food was beans (soup beans or Pinto beans), potatoes, and cornbread. In the summer, we ate many vegetables out of the garden. I could take a saltshaker and go into the garden hungry and come out stuffed. We ate beans and potatoes six days a week and sometimes seven. I never got tired of it and still love it to this day.

If there were any beans left over after a couple or three days, Maw would drain the soup off into a container and squash the beans and make fried bean cakes. This is the hillbilly version of Mexican refried beans. If there were any potatoes left over, she would squash them down and make fried potato cakes. I have eaten these fried beans and potato cakes many, many times. They are good—really good! Maw could make killer fried apple pies also.

I hope this does not sound like I am complaining. I am not. I am very thankful for what I had. I never ever remember going to bed hungry. There are many people that can't say that. Thank you, Lord.

When I was growing up, I had three chores to do every day, seven days a week. The first chore was to keep the drinking water bucket in the house full. On wash day, I had to draw three washtubs full of water from the well.

The second chore was to keep the kindling wood box behind the stove full so that Maw had dry wood to build a fire in the cooking stove anytime she wanted. Also, I had to keep the woodshed full for winter. My third chore was to keep the coal bucket full of small lump coal. Once, Maw built a fire with the wood. Coal was added, and we had a good fire. Coal was added as needed all day long. I had to make sure the coal shed was full before winter set in.

As I got older, I was given more responsibility, such as fixing the roof, windows, painting, and anything else that needed fixing.

In the summer, I did a lot of hoeing in the garden. This wasn't work to me. I enjoyed watching the plants grow. I also had to keep the fence in pretty good shape to keep Granny Rowe's cow out.

I also had to keep the grass and weeds cut. In the wintertime, after supper, Maw would let the fire in the cooking stove die out. This saved on the coal supply. The heating stove was in the living room and gave out quite a lot of heat. But it was not enough heat to take care of the whole house. The living room was comfortable, but that was about it.

When we got ready to go to bed, Maw would bank the fire down. This was done so there would be fire in the stove in the morning. To bank the fire, you shut the draft. This cuts off the air supply to the fire. Then, you have to put a great deal of coal on top of the fire, mostly slack coal. The slack coal is a fine powdered coal about like sand. This slack coal slowed the fire down. It didn't take long for the house to get cold. After a couple of hours, the house temperature dropped to the same temperature as outside. If the temperature got below 32 degrees, the water in the water bucket froze. If you wanted some water to make coffee or maybe brush your teeth, you had to break the ice to get the water. You had no problem getting a cold drink of water. If the wind was blowing and it was snowing, the curtains above my bed would stand out. In the morning, there would be a light skiff of snow on my bed.

If it got very cold out, we would put all the blankets we had on the bed.

Also, we would take the throw rugs off the floor and put them on the bed. When we got in bed, the covers were so heavy it was almost work to turn over in the bed. I would put on three pairs of socks to keep my feet warm. I know this sounds unbelievable, but it is true.

Maw always got up first every morning. She would open the draft and shake the grate. The grate was a heavy piece of flat cast iron with holes in it. When you shake it back and forth, all the dead ashes fall through the cracks and this allows more air to get to the fire. After Maw shook the grate, she would open the door of the stove and use a poker to stir the fire up. It didn't take long, and the heating stove was putting out heat and doing its job. Then, she would go to the kitchen and build a fire in the cooking stove. Sometimes, when the wood was a little damp, she would use about a half a cup of kerosene to help get it going. Occasionally, the fire was just about out, and she wanted to get it going, so she would sprinkle a little bit of sugar on it. Pretty soon, it would be blazing.

After she got the fire in the heating stove going and it was going pretty well, I would jump out of bed. It was so cold that your feet stuck to the linoleum floor. I would grab my clothes and run into the living room and get behind the stove. That was the warmest place in the house. Usually, by the time I got dressed, Maw had breakfast ready. I can still recall the smell of the wood burning and the smell of breakfast. This all sounds really bad, and some of it was. But all in all, those were some of the best days of my life, and I wouldn't trade them for anything.

Telephone Poles

Our house where I lived was located at the mouth of Horn Holler. Up in the holler was one other house and the large fan that belonged to the coal company I mentioned previously. Either the electric company or the coal company decided to put new electric poles up the holler. The electric poles are treated with creosote; this makes them last for years and years. The creosote burns very good.

They took the old poles down and replaced them with bigger, newer poles. They took all the old poles with them except one that was only about 200 feet from my house. One of my main chores was to have enough firewood chopped up and stored in the woodshed to last all winter.

I kept my eye on the electric pole that was left behind. It kept looking better and better. After about a year or two, I decided nobody wanted it. If they had of wanted it, they would have taken it. So, I sawed it up in about one-foot pieces and hauled it home in my trusty wagon. When I got home, I split it up into kindling and put it in the woodshed.

I had a friend who had a bucksaw. It worked good on the pole. It really helped fill the shed. During the summer, any kind of wood I could drag home and cut up, I did. If I didn't have the shed full by late fall, I had to go up in the mountains and drag home enough wood to finish filling the shed.

Maybe two or three months later, my Uncle Tom came to me and asked me if I knew what happened to the electric pole that was laying on the ground.

As bad as I hated to, I had to tell him I cut it up and put it in the wood-shed. I also told him it had been laying up there for a couple of years and I didn't think anyone wanted it. I was grasping at straws trying to make my case look good. Now I know what George Washington felt like when he was confronted about the cherry tree.

He told me they came up in the holler looking for it but couldn't find it. They were going to use it someplace. He left, and that was the last I heard about the electric pole. He might have had to pay for it, but I don't know. I do know it sure came in handy that winter.

Fire in the House

The house we lived in was very old. It was probably one of the first ones built when the mine first opened.

Insulation probably had not been invented at the time the house was built. There was no insulation anywhere in the house. The sheet rock on the walls had large gaps where they were not butted up tight together and had never been taped. So, in turn, there were some places where you could see inside the walls, and you could see the underside of the roof. If you looked where the roof came down and met the walls, you could see daylight and wasp nests with wasps working on them.

One winter night, my sister, Sue; my mother, Ett; and Maw were home. I don't know where I was that particular night. In the middle of the night, my sister woke up and the house was full of smoke. She immediately jumped out of bed and woke up Ett and Maw. She told them the house was on fire.

After Ett and Maw had gotten up and were making their way to the door, they looked up through the cracks in the sheet rock and could see fire up in the attic around the chimney. Ett put her finger in one of the cracks and pulled a large piece of sheet rock down.

The fire was almost all the way around the chimney. The underside of the roof was burning.

We always had a water bucket full of water in the kitchen. There was always a water dipper hanging on the wall right above the water bucket.

Everyone used the dipper when we wanted a drink. No one thought a thing about using the dipper and drinking after someone else. If we had company, they drank with the same dipper.

My sister grabbed the water bucket and dipper and took it into the living room. She hurriedly started throwing dippers full of water on the fire.

We had a well in the back yard. Ett ran out to the well and got another bucket full of water. By the time Ett got back into the house with the bucket, Sue's bucket was about empty. But Sue continued to throw dippers of water on it.

The fire was starting to die down a little bit. Ett quickly changed buckets with Sue and went speeding back to the well. When she got back with that bucket full, the fire was almost out.

After they got the fire out, they were afraid to go back to bed. They sat up the rest of the night. The next day, Tom came over and surveyed the damage to the house. Then, Tom got a brick layer to fix the chimney.

Three or four weeks later, everyone in the holler knew about the fire. The superintendent of the mine had found out and came to the house. He thanked Sue for her quick thinking and gave her a five-dollar bill.

I thought that was nice of him to thank my sister. I am sure my sister used the five dollars wisely.

When Sue was at home, she made potato soup. When you only had potatoes in the house, you made do with whatever you had. If I remember correctly, it goes kind of like this: Dice the potatoes and place them in a pot and just cover them with water. Add a half of a stick of butter to the pot. Then, you add some salt and pepper to taste. Boil until the potatoes are soft. Next, remove the pot from the heat. Add condensed milk and continue to stir a great deal.

When she made it, it was great!

Harvey

All the way up at the head of Patterson holler was an old house. You probably could call it a shack. A couple lived there, and they had a six- or seven-year-old son named Harvey. Every day, rain or shine, Harvey walked about three miles to school. He had to pass our house on his way going and coming.

I don't know how my grandmother found out that Harvey was going to school every day without having anything to eat. I knew that when Harvey walked by it was hurting Maw. A few days after she found out about Harvey, she sat out on the porch and waited for Harvey to come down the holler. As she sat there, she would look up the holler every minute or two watching for him. Pretty soon, she saw him coming, and she went out to the road and got him. She brought him in and sat him down at the kitchen table and fixed him breakfast and continued to do that every morning from then on. Maw told me, "We don't have much, but we have enough for one more." Maw could not stand for anything, human or animal, to go hungry.

Harvey's dad was paralyzed from the waist down. I never saw him in a wheelchair. Owning a wheelchair was for rich people. There wasn't any money for a wheelchair in this family.

90% of the time when you passed their house, the old man was out in the garden. He would sit in the dirt and drag himself from plant to plant.

His main tool was a hoe with about a three-foot handle. The old man was doing all he could to feed his family.

The garden was huge. Every row was perfectly straight. There was not one weed in the whole garden. His garden would have made the front page of "Better Homes and Gardens." I wish I had helped them in some way, but when you are a kid most things go over your head.

Sometimes during the winter, Harvey's mother would walk from her house down the holler and go from door to door asking for food. When she came to our house, Maw always gave her something. She never left our house empty handed.

My grandmother was a "Wonder Woman" in so many ways. She did so much with so little for so long. She could take nothing and do anything.

Maw raised eight children and half a dozen grandchildren on beans and potatoes.

Gold Key

One of my friends—I'll call him Buddy—was a few years older than me. About once a month, Buddy asked me if I was going to be busy on Friday or Saturday night. Most of the time, the only thing I did on the weekends was watch wrestling on Saturday night. He would let me know when and what day. In addition, he would urge me to go party with him.

When the day came, he would stop and pick me up, and we would go to Garden Creek. There was a beer joint there called the "Gold Key." The building was on ground level. When you walked in, there were a few bar stools, three or four tables, and chairs.

Downstairs, they had a dance floor, tables, and chairs. On the weekend, they had a band playing country and western music. They always had a good band.

Buddy and I would go downstairs, and he would drink beer. I was too young to buy beer, so I would drink Pepsi or Coke. It was a miracle I did not OD on sugar. At that time, you couldn't buy hard liquor across the bar—only beer.

On Friday and Saturday night, there was always a bootlegger in the parking lot selling liquor by the pint.

Buddy would drink and dance with all the ladies—no certain one. He would always ask the man if he cared if he asked his lady friend to dance. We always stayed until the band quit playing and they unplugged the juke box. Buddy was always a gentleman and never caused any trouble. When it was time to leave, he always gave me the keys to drive home. I was too young to have a driver's license. He said it would be a lot cheaper to pay a "no driver's license" ticket than a DWI ticket.

Thanks for the good times, Buddy. Rest in peace.

Drive-In

One weekend, my friend Junior and I were looking for something to do. There wasn't much of anything going on in Patterson. We got the bright idea that we would ride our bikes down to Vansant and go to the drive-in movies. Vansant was 10 or 12 miles down the road toward Grundy. When you get to Vansant, you turn left across the bridge, and the drive-in was right there. We didn't take any water or anything to eat. A great deal of planning didn't go into this trip. All we had was two old rag bicycles and the want to. We did good going down there. We did a lot of coasting. Common sense should tell you that if you coast one way, you will have to peddle the other. When we got down there, we hid our bikes and crawled under the fence. We found us a good spot and watched the movie.

Now, all we had to do was ride home. We slid back under the fence and retrieved our bikes and headed back up to Patterson. After a couple of miles, it seemed like the bikes were gaining weight. After another mile or two, we decided to push our bikes and give them a rest. The farther we went, the harder the bikes were to push. We decided to stop and let the bikes rest some more. Occasionally, we would get to ride down a little slope. There were a lot more upslopes than downslopes. While we were letting the bikes rest again, we decided this was going to be work. There had to be a better way.

Change of plans. We decided to hide the bikes, hitchhike home, and come back for the bikes later. We hid the bikes over the side of the hill.

We decided we would walk toward the holler while we were hitchhiking. At 12:00 at night, there aren't too many cars headed up to Patterson. It is almost impossible to hitchhike with no cars going by. Hitchhike contains two words. "Hitch" means to catch a ride. "Hike" means to walk. We walked the rest of the way home.

We learned a valuable lesson. It is a hell of a lot easier to ride a bike down to Vansant than it is to ride a bike from Vansant up to Patterson. Junior and I never tried that trick again. We did go back and get our bikes.

We went to the drive-in many times after that. But we always rode a car through the front gate. Most of the time, we were in the trunk.

Boots

When most of the kids started school each fall, most of us got a new pair of shoes to wear to school. When they got home after school, they had to take them off until the next morning. As the school year went on, the new shoes became old shoes.

When my shoes got old and holes in the soles, I would put pieces of tar paper inside my shoes. If I didn't put the tar paper in the bottom and I stepped on a penny I could tell if it was heads or tails. In school, I would always keep my feet flat on the floor, and I never crossed my legs. I didn't want anyone to see the holes in my shoes.

My Uncle Harry was involved in a serious accident. He was in really bad shape for a long time. He spent about three months in the hospital and months in rehabilitation. When he was released from the hospital, one of his legs was 1 ½ inches shorter than the other. He had special shoes and boots made. He visited us and when he left, he left a good pair of boots, except one heel was 1 ½ inches higher than the other. We let him know he left them at Maw's house. He wrote us a letter and said he would get them when he came back. At that time, I did not have any shoes or work boots, either. His boots fit me perfectly except for the heel. I started wearing them. By the time school started, I could walk in them without limping. I think I was in the 10th grade. I wore them all school year, and no one ever knew.

When I had gym, I put on tennis shoes and always put my shoes back under the bench so no one would kick them over. That would have been very embarrassing.

Herman and Omie

One of my Maw's sisters was named Omie. She was married to Herman Proffitt. They had four or five children, all of whom were older than me. I stayed with them one winter.

Two of his boys worked in the coal mines, but not in Patterson. All their girls were married and gone.

Herman worked for the Sycamore Coal Company in Patterson. He was a motor man. His job was the same as an engineer on the railroad, except he pulled small, empty cars into the mine. Then, he hauled the filled cars back out of the mine. The cars ran on a small railroad track. When he pulled the filled cars out of the mine, he went around to the head house and dumped them there. The coal then went down the mountain to the tipple where it was processed and put in railroad cars to be shipped.

Herman was known for stretching the truth just a little bit. In hillbilly slang, he was known as being "windy."

Herman was really a nice guy, and he would do anything for anyone. Also, he never stretched the truth about anyone other than himself. One of the miners said Herman was windier than a sack full of buttholes.

Omie was a good ole gal. Also, she would help you out if you needed it.

She made the best homemade biscuits that I have ever had. I know good biscuits when I have one. When she made them, she used pure lard. You could eat her three-day-old biscuits just like they were baked that morning.

Herman got Black Lung from the coal dust in the mine. He passed away. Omie has since passed away also. She smoked a lot of cigarettes. Maybe the cigarettes had something to do with her death.

Thanks for letting me stay there with you for one winter. Rest in peace.

Flint, Michigan

One day, in late fall or early spring, I was piddling around at the house doing nothing constructive, as usual. My friend, Junior, came down to my house and stopped. He was driving his dad's 1956 Chevy. He said he and his dad had a few words, and they weren't seeing eye to eye.

So, he decided to leave, and he stopped to see if I wanted to go with him. I asked where he wanted to go. He replied, "Let's go to Florida." That was all he had to say. I instantly saw sandy beaches, the ocean, and dozens of bikini-clad, sun-tanned girls. You know I wanted to go. My biggest decision was paper or plastic. It only took a split second to tell him, "Yes." I told him to wait till I got all my crap in one sack. I scraped up all the money I could find. It couldn't have been very much. I gathered up all my clean and cleanest dirty clothes. I threw them in a brown paper suitcase, and away we went. At that time, I had not been more than a 100-mile radius from the holler in my life.

We probably ran one or two tanks of gas out before we woke up and discovered we were going north instead of south. Maybe it was when we crossed the Ohio River. I realized I had never seen a river that big in my life.

This Florida plan isn't working at all. We better get a new set of blueprints.

One of our friends, Bobby had broken out of the holler and was working in Flint, Michigan. After much discussion between Junior and I, we decided to go to Flint and bunk in with Bobby. Then, we would get a job. We had gone too far north, and we had too much invested to turn back now. We traded Florida for Flint.

We went through one city, and red lights were everywhere! I didn't think there were that many red lights in the whole United States.

I thought it was cold here when we left Patterson. The further north we went, the colder it got. We only had summer clothes. No need to take a coat if you are going to Florida. All we were going to need was a pair of cutoffs and a T-shirt.

After at least half a million miles, we made it to Flint, Michigan. Flint was a city and not some wide place in the road. In those days, there were not any GPS units or cellphones. For a couple of hillbillies that didn't know shit from Shinola, much less north from south, we were damn lucky to even find Flint. We actually found where Bobby worked. That was nothing short of a miracle.

The guys that worked there said Bobby had left there days before. He was headed to Patterson, Virginia. We had passed him somewhere on the way.

It was colder than a deep freezer. The weather was going from bad to worse. It was pouring snow. This was the first time I had ever seen it snow sideways. The wind was blowing so hard it would shake the car. I had heard about a blizzard and read about them. Now, I know what they really are.

We spent the night in the car. We were lucky we didn't fall asleep and not wake up. It could have happened very easy. It was miserable. I don't think it quit snowing or blowing all night. The next morning, we had some decisions to make. We could stay there and wait on Bobby to get back or to go back home. The decision was definitely a no-brainer. We were headed South.

The snow was still coming down and sideways. This was a real snowstorm.

If we would have had the least bit of car trouble, we would have frozen to death. It was a miracle we didn't have an accident on that snow covered road.

We were doing pretty good. Then, we got pulled over in Marion, Ohio for running a red light. They made us follow them to the police station. They gave us the third degree.

Junior had to show them the insurance papers. There was also some mail in the glovebox addressed to Junior's dad, Henry. After what seemed like a hundred hours, they decided to let us go without giving us a ticket. They probably felt sorry for a couple of hillbilly boys.

When we crossed the Virginia state line, I could have gotten out of the car and kissed the ground. I sure was glad to be back in my home state.

We got within a few miles of home, and the rear end of the car went out. Thank you, Lord, for not letting us break down in Michigan.

Our Guardian Angels were working overtime on that excursion.

Moonshine

My friend, Junior, and I were broke all the time. We didn't have two nickels to rub together. Times were tough for a couple of hillbilly boys. You couldn't beg, borrow, steal, or buy a job—not even a little handyman job. Desperate times called for desperate measures.

We know people drink to celebrate their good fortunes, and they drink to drown their sorrows. They also drink a lot in between. We decided we would go into business bootlegging (selling moonshine).

We knew an old man up on Bradshaw Mountain who used to sell moonshine. He had quit selling when the Federales came snooping around. We decided to go over to Bradshaw Mountain and pay him a visit. Maybe he was back in business or knew someone who was and could introduce us to them. A stranger could not buy a drop of liquor if his life depended on it.

If you are not in, you are definitely out.

We went over to his house and sat on the porch. He remembered us from a while back. We proceeded to tell him what we were after and could he help us out. His first words were after he wiped the smile off his face and answered, "You all came to the right place."

He told us that when the Federales came around, he did not quit. He wanted everyone to think he had quit. He just moved his still to a different location.

I think we bought five gallons for $21.25, or $4.25 per gallon. We paid for them and loaded them in the car. We were getting ready to leave, and the old man guaranteed us we would not get caught from his house to the West Virginia/Virginia state line. But once we crossed into Virginia, we were on our own. We did not ask any questions, but we thanked him. We made it back to Patterson without a problem. Now the real work would begin.

We went to all the trash dumps up and down the creek. We also traveled up and down the roads and ditches. We were looking for pint bottles. We had to clean the bottles and make sure they had a good lid or cap so they would not leak.

We cleaned the bottles good and made sure they were dry. When we filled the pint bottles, we made sure we did not spill a drop. We didn't want to short anyone. We had to get eight pints per gallon. If we sold them for two dollars per pint, that would give us a net profit of $58.75. There aren't many businesses that turn a profit the first week.

The first pint we sold, disaster struck. Junior handed it to the guy but dropped it before the guy had it in his hand. It hit the black-top road and shattered into a million pieces. That cost $2.00. It was a severe blow to our bottom line. We sold all we had. Most everyone who bought it said it was good liquor.

We went back for a second load. When we got to his house and told him what we wanted, he told us to sit down and wait. He would go get it. We sat on the porch, and he disappeared into the trees. About 20 or 25 minutes passed, and then you could hear him coming. He was carrying jugs of liquor in a feed sack.

The sound of the jugs of liquor bumping together is a very distinct sound. Once you have heard it, you won't forget it. It is like someone cocking a gun. I often wondered why the jugs of liquor didn't break, but they never did. When he got back to the porch, he was huffing and puffing. He sat on the porch for a while to catch his breath. He told us he was going to give us a lesson in reading the proof of moonshine. You take one of the half gallon liquor jugs and turn it upside down. Then, you turn it right side up. Some of the bubbles come to the top and form a chain between the glass jug and the liquor. Part of the bubble will be above the liquor, and part of the bubble will be under the liquor. The amount that the bubble is above the liquor tells you what proof it is.

The moonshine that we just bought was 100 proof.

We paid for the liquor with cash. No credit card, no check, and absolutely no credit. This was strictly a cash-and-carry business.

My Uncle Harry gave me a 1950 Ford four-door standard shift. That was my first car. Looking back on the car, it was a rag. But it was my rag, free and clear, and I had the title for it. The motor was the best part of the whole car. It had four slick "may pop" tires (may pop any time).

One evening, we were getting low on stock. Business was good. We were selling a lot of product. We decided to go over the mountain and get five gallons of liquor. Usually, we tried to slip away when we were going to get liquor. Two of the other boys wanted to ride along. This was the first time we had passengers. We always went by ourselves.

We got over there and made a purchase without any problem. We might have bought a half gallon extra. As soon as we cleared the old man's house, we broke the seal on one of the jugs. This was also a first. We never drank while we were hauling a load.

By the time we got off Bradshaw Mountain and down Slate Creek to the post office where we turned left off the main road, the moonshine was doing its job. By that point, no one was feeling any pain.

The road across the mountain to Patterson was rough—real rough in some places. It seemed like it was a 45-degree incline. The road was rutted out pretty bad, too.

The old Ford was in first gear, easing up the mountain. The motor was purring like a kitten. When the road had deep ruts, you tried to stay on the high places with the tires so the car didn't drag or get stuck. Junior and I had been across the mountain at least a dozen times with no problems. We were steadily climbing. The moonshine was tasting better and better. Moonshine is rough to drink at first, but after a while it smooths out and goes down like water. By now, all four of us were higher than a Georgia pine. The old Ford was still in low gear cranking at a high rate of RPMs. About another half mile, and we would cross over the top. Then, it would be smooth sailing on down to Patterson.

Disaster strikes when you drink and drive on mountain roads like we were on. You are asking for trouble, and if you aren't careful, you will get it.

We were getting close to the top when the old Ford slid off the high side and went down in the rut. Once you are down, it is hard to climb back up on the high side. The old Ford was dragging every inch of the way. The muffler couldn't stand the strain of all the dragging, so it was the first thing to go. Instantly, the noise was off the chart. The motor was still cranking at a high rate of RPMs. It sounded like the motor was having labor pains. It was screaming.

The muffler was laying on the ground back behind us. It was the only one I had. I didn't want to buy a new one. I had no choice but to stop. I know you know that moonshine is clear, but it clouds the thinking. The more you drink, the cloudier the thinking gets.

As soon as I stopped, one of the boys in the backseat jumped out and said he would get it. Billy ran back and grabbed the muffler with both hands. It was rather heavy. If it would've been daylight, I am sure you would have seen smoke come off both of his hands. As soon as he touched it, the damage was done. He couldn't turn it loose fast enough. Both of his hands were scorched. He should have gone to the hospital, but he didn't go. Hospitals cost money. The other boy in the back stuck a stick in the outlet of the muffler and picked it up. He had to put it in the floorboard of the backseat. We couldn't take the chance of putting it in the trunk and it rolling around and breaking a jug of liquor. We made it back to Patterson that night with only one wounded.

Junior and I were doing pretty good in the liquor business. We had money to spend and money in our pockets for the first time ever. It was a good feeling to know that if we wanted a bottle of pop or to go to the movies, we could afford it. Thank you, Lord.

We had quite a few regular customers. Sometimes, we would extend them a little credit. When payday rolled around, we got our money. The holler is small, and you see most of the people just about every day.

One of our best customers' wives sent someone to find us to tell us she wanted to talk to us. Oh crap! We imagined a thousand things that she could have wanted to talk to us about. We decided no matter what it was, it can't be good for us. This could have been the end of our lucrative business careers. We put it off as long as we could. But sooner or later, we had to face her.

The day of judgment was upon us. We went to her house and pecked on the door. When she answered the door, she did not have a gun in her hand or any other thing she could have used to inflict bodily harm. That was the first good thing so far. She invited us in and motioned for us to have a seat on the couch. I thought maybe she was going to get us in the house, lock the door, and there would be no place to run. She offered us a glass of water. I think I could've spit dust right about then. I said, "No, thank you." She sat down in a chair directly across from us so she could look us straight in our eyes. She didn't beat around the bush and got straight to the point. She wanted to know if we would loan her enough money to buy her daughter a pair of shoes. I didn't know about Junior, but I got about 50 pounds lighter. If I remember correctly, she wanted the new shoes so her daughter could go to Sunday school and church on Easter Sunday. We gave her the money and told her to forget about paying us back. The lady did not know it, but she could have asked to borrow enough money for a half a dozen pair of shoes, and she would have gotten it.

When I walked out of her house, I was on cloud nine. Oh, what a relief it was! I think I heard Junior singing.

The moonshine business was getting better and better. We decided to expand our empire. We would take a bunch to Grundy and sell it there. On Friday and Saturday, the town was packed with people, especially if it was on the 1st or the 15th of the month. That was when the miners got paid. We stuffed our clothes with as many pints as we could conceal. Then, we went to the Morgan Theatre. We sold every pint we had and could have sold more. We probably made more money than the concession stand. Many people staggered out of the theatre when the movie was over. I think we only did this once, maybe twice. I think we got cold feet because of the police in town. We made good money in the theatre. But staying out of jail was a lot better.

Everything was going good for us. We found a steady source of pint bottles. They had been used. The only thing we had to do was pick them up, haul them home, put them in a tub of boiling water for a few minutes, and rinse them off. We had to let them dry, and then they were ready to be filled. However, all good things come to an end usually sooner rather than later. We did not know it, but our moonshine days were drawing to a close.

I lived at the mouth of Horn Holler. It was a small holler running off the main road in Patterson. Junior and I had a small fortune in pints of moonshine hidden in that holler and surrounding mountains. It was just waiting to be turned into cash.

One day, Junior came down and told me his dad wanted to see me. Slice this any way you want to; it can't be good. The pressure is on, big time. We take our time getting up to Junior's house. Henry is waiting on the front porch. I can't hardly look at him—definitely not eye to eye. I looked at the trees, porch floor, and anywhere but at him. I know I had guilt written all over me in capital letters. Ray Charles could see that.

Once he started talking to us, I could tell he wasn't mad by the tone of his voice. That was one point in our favor. He started telling us that we were going to get into big trouble if we kept on selling the moonshine. He stressed the point that if one wrong person, or some guy's wife got mad and dropped a dime on us, it would be all over. We would have a police record for the rest of our lives.

He said he would like for us to stop before we went to jail. Once we get caught, it would be too late. We agree with him and told him we would as soon as we sold our inventory. We had quite a bit of product stashed everywhere.

We told him we wouldn't buy any more, and we didn't. At the end of our conversation, the last thing he said was, "Do you boys have a spare pint?" Of course, we immediately obliged and got him one. Junior and I never went back to the bootlegger's place again together.

About two years later, I made two trips to the bootlegger's house by myself. He wasn't there either time. When I asked where he was, I got two different stories.

I don't know which story was correct or if either one of them was true. You can make up your own mind.

When I made the first trip to get a load, the bootlegger's wife told me he was in jail. The ATF had gotten him. A few years before, he had told us we didn't have to worry while we were in West Virginia. Whether he was in jail or not, the moonshine had not stopped flowing.

During the second trip, some man I had never seen before did the deal. I got a little nervous dealing with someone I didn't know. When I asked him about the bootlegger, the story he told me was pretty wild. He said the old man had his mule and sled back in the mountains. The old man always carried a .38 Smith & Wesson revolver in the front of his pants. The mule decided to stop to take a rest, and the old man started hollering at the mule and was hitting it on the rump with the leather straps. The mule did not move. Somehow the old man got between the mule and the sled. When he did, the mule jerked the sled and knocked the old man down. The sled had sideboards on it and were held by long staves, or pieces of wood, sticking up. One of the pieces of wood hit the trigger on the .38 and shot a hole through the old man's *you know what!* When the gun went off, the noise startled the mule. The mule took off and dragged the sled over top of the old man. Between the gun shot and the sled, it allegedly put the old man in the hospital in critical condition. He was getting better, but it was a slow process.

I never saw the old man again, so I can't say which story was true or if either one was.

The last two loads, I hauled to Ohio and sold them at the Ford plant in Lorain, Ohio. That was the end of running moonshine for me.

Coca-Cola Glasses

Late one night in the fall, four or five of us boys had been to a football game at the Garden Creek High School. After the game was over, we decided to go to a drive-in restaurant about two or three miles up in Garden Creek. Many girls hung out there. One of the guys from Garden Creek had bought a 1956 Chevrolet convertible. It was two-tone black and mint green. That was a beautiful car. It was the envy of all the boys. When you had a daydream, this car was what it was about.

After we had been up there for quite a while, it was getting late, and we decided to go home.

We were almost down to the intersection of Garden Creek and Route 460 when it happened. We ran out of gas.

We had to spring into action. Plan A was to walk to a gas station and buy a couple of gallons of gas. At this time of night, all the gas stations were closed. Scrap Plan A. Go to Plan B and borrow a couple of gallons. We did not know anyone well enough to beat on their door at this time of night. Scrap Plan B. Go to Plan C, and break out the can and siphoning hose. Desperate times called for desperate measures.

The closest place to get some gas was the school buses at Garden Creek High School. There were a half a dozen buses there, and they all had gas. We were sure they wouldn't miss a couple of gallons.

I think three of us were elected to go borrow the gas. One of us was called "Heavy Duty." He wore glasses that were three or four notches past coke bottles. We were all scared to death we'd get caught, or worse—shot!

We located one bus without a locked gas cap. Everything was running well.

One of the boys panicked and said he thought he saw someone coming.

It was time to go. Someone grabbed the hose out of the bus. Heavy Duty grabbed one side of the can, and someone else grabbed the other side. With one on one side and one on the other, you can run a lot faster with the can in the middle.

Back then, the milk was delivered to schools in wire-mesh crates. They were strong and unforgiving. Everyone was running as fast as they could. Heavy Duty stepped in one of the crates at full throttle. He went down like he was shot. The gas can went rolling down the parking lot, spilling gas at every rotation after rotation after rotation.

In about 15 seconds, everything went from going pretty well to three boys on their hands and knees looking for a pair of glasses. As soon as we found the glasses and retrieved the can, we could take off again.

We managed to save enough gas to get us home. Heavy Duty had road rash on both hands, and he limped around for a couple of weeks. His glasses were just fine. I never heard him complain one time. He said his hands and foot would heal, but his glasses wouldn't. If his glasses had been broken or scratched, he would've had to go to the eye doctor to get them repaired or buy a new pair. I am sure he would've had to take someone with him to be a co-signer to help him pay for them.

That was the last time we ever ran out of gas. We got away with it one time. We didn't push our luck.

Heart Operation

J unior and I made the big decision that we were going to join the Air
Force. I can't remember how we got to the induction center. It was
located in Roanoke, Virginia. That was a long way from home. It surprised me how many people were there taking the tests. Both of us passed
the written exams with flying colors. Then, we went for the physical. They
lined everyone up, and you stripped down to your bloomers. They didn't
miss a thing, front or back. They made you drop your drawers and bend over
and spread your cheeks—yes, those cheeks.

One of the things we had to do was run in place to get our heart pumping.
They came down the line and listened to our hearts. They listened to mine, then
went on down the line. They didn't catch my little problem, or so I thought.
One by one, they called out your name. They called out Junior's name. They
kept calling out names, and pretty soon I was the only one standing in line. They
told me to get my clothes on and follow them. We went to another room, and
I had to get up on the table. Maybe four or five doctors checked my heart. They
told me I had a heart problem and to go home, and I would hear from them.

About a week later, my Uncle Harry got a call. I had an appointment at
the University of Virginia in Charlottesville, and I'd better not miss it.

When the appointment rolled around, Harry took me. I was there on time,
front and center. They took me in and asked me a million questions about
my family, smoking, drinking, and everything. They documented everything.

Then, I went to another room, and they put me upon a table for the next two hours. One doctor after another came in and listened to my heart. There was question after question. About noon, they turned me loose and told me to come back the next day at 9 o'clock in the morning. I went the next day and had to go to a different room. In that room, there was a big plastic replica of a heart. It was almost as big as a basketball. Two doctors came in, and as they took the heart apart, they explained to me about each part. They showed me what they thought was my problem. I needed a heart operation quick.

They told me that if I had a heart operation, I had a 50/50 chance of making it, and if I did not have the operation, I would not live to see my 21st birthday. Also, they said I had lived longer than anyone they ever knew about with this problem. I was living on borrowed time. This did not sound too promising to me.

I told them that I didn't have any money for an operation, and I did not have a job. There was no way I could afford this, so they sent me home. I went back to my same old routine. About two weeks later, my uncle got a call from the University of Virginia Hospital. They had scheduled me for a heart operation the following week. I did want to keep the appointment.

This was music to my ears. Yes, I kept the appointment. When you are 17 or 18 years old, you think you are bulletproof, so the 50/50 survival rate did not bother me one bit. Someone had talked to the Heart Foundation, and they were going to pay 100% of the bill. Thank you! Thank you! Thank you!

The day I got there, I was placed in the room. Then, one of the doctors came in and asked me if I cared if they brought some interns in to listen to my heart. For what they were doing for me, they could've brought the whole hospital staff in. About 20 young interns came in and listened to my heart.

Heart operations were not a common thing like they are today. The procedure has come a long way in 60+ years.

My big day came. They had to cancel it because I was underage and had to have a legal guardian. My Uncle Harry got a lawyer and drew up the papers, and he signed for me. Okay, my big day is here again. The hospital had to cancel it again. They did not have enough of my blood type, which was AB-. Maybe the good Lord was trying to tell me something. My big day was now the next day. At 6 a.m. the next morning, I was prepped, and I received a shot to calm me down. By the time they wheeled me down the hall, I was happy, happy, happy! Whatever it was, it worked.

There was a funeral home in Grundy. The very first person I saw when I woke up was the guy that drove the hurst for the funeral home. I assumed they sent him to Charlottesville to pick me up. But I did not die. He had to travel back to Grundy with an empty meat wagon. I was not sorry about that.

At the University of Virginia where I was, there were about 360 student nurses. I didn't see an ugly one in the whole bunch. One of them was assigned to me to write her term paper. She came to see me every day and usually asked a bunch of questions. Then, she would write down all my responses. After I could get around with no tubes attached, I slipped out of the hospital. I was clothed only in my little hospital gown and was barefooted. I met her across the street at a little ice cream shop. I do not remember what we had, but I do recall she paid the tab. I felt bad about her paying the bill.

I was in the hospital for 11 days in a semi-private room. The guy in the room with me was Willie Chewning. He was a barber in Bland, Virginia. We got to be pretty good friends.

One day, I took a stroll down the hall, and when I got back to the room, there were three or four doctors and a couple of nurses working on him. He was hooked up to a machine that looked like a giant thermometer. Every time he had a heartbeat, the mercury would hit the top of the gauge.

I went back out in the hall for a while. In about 15 minutes, they got his blood pressure under control. He had heart surgery also. He was still there when I was released. I never heard from him again. Hopefully, he made it.

Dr. Blank did my surgery, and he did a great job. The Heart Foundation paid for it 100%. I owe them big time. They are in my will. I hope there will be something left for them. My wife also sends them a little donation twice a year.

Beer Joint Outhouse

If you don't have a strong stomach, you might want to skip this chapter. It is rather bizarre and wild. 99% of the things written in this book happened, and I was there to witness them. This chapter, I was not there. The story was told to me by a miner. He was a few years older than me and was a straight shooter. He had nothing to gain by lying about it. Also, I heard the same story a few days later from another guy. I do think it happened.

The story is being told as it was told to me, as close as I can recall.

If you were on Route 460 going from Grundy to Richlands, you would travel through a small coal mining community called Keen Mountain. At that time, there were two or three beer joints around that area. No whiskey across the bar was allowed. It was against the law.

Jim was in one of the beer joints (sometimes referred to as beer gardens). He was having a good time drinking, playing the jukebox and shooting pool. He probably knew all the people in the joint. Jim spent a lot of time there. You could call him a regular. There was one lady there. I am not going to say she was fat. He said she could shade you in the summer and keep you warm in the winter. She was big enough that her boyfriend could kiss on her all night and never kiss the same place twice. In other words, she passed petite when she was 10 years old.

Everyone was having a great time. The music was loud, and the beer was flowing.

Suddenly, everyone was going outside. The entire beer joint was emptying out fast. The only reason everyone would go outside was if there was a fight. You weren't allowed to fight inside the beer joint. No one wanted to miss a good fight. Jim was one of the last ones out of the joint. When he got outside, everyone was ganged up around the outhouse. Jim said he couldn't believe it. He had never seen a fight in the shithouse. Maybe someone jumped in front of the line.

He was accurate. There was not a fight happening. What was really going on soon revealed itself. The well-endowed lady had stepped into the outhouse to wring it out. The floor gave way, and down she went! They could not get her back up through the floor.

They had to remove the outhouse from over the hole. It was a great deal of work, and the outhouse was not in the best condition either. She did not get hurt. She just received a few scratches here and there. The only thing that really got hurt was her pride, and she was very embarrassed to say the least.

Lawsuits were almost unheard of back then. Nowadays, that incident would be worth millions.

One thing is for sure—she sure made a big stink that night!

You couldn't call rescue squads back then. If you could, they probably wouldn't have answered that call.

Epilogue

This will be the last chapter of my life and travels growing up in and around the holler known as Patterson, Virginia.

If I embarrassed anyone or told any family secrets, then I am sorry. It wasn't intentional. There are a few stories that should be left untold. I tried to stay away from the real eyeopeners, and there are a few.

Any one of the boys who grew up in the holler could tell some interesting stories. We were all in the same boat.

You can take the boy out of the mountains, but you can't take the mountains out of the boy

I have been a hillbilly for 80+ years and will continue to be for the duration of my life. A lot of water has passed under the bridge in those 80 years. Much of it was cloudy, and much was crystal clear. I have been blessed more than any one person should be.

A few more years, and the few of us that are still here pass on. All the memories of the good times and bad times that made Patterson will be forgotten. For me, that is very sad.

If I kick the bucket today, I can honestly say beyond a shadow of a doubt that it has been a good ride.

Thank you, Lord.

CPSIA information can be obtained
at www.ICGtesting.com
Printed in the USA
JSHW010913130423
40240JS00005B/27